THE XERISCAPE FLOWER GARDENER

A WATERWISE GUIDE FOR THE ROCKY MOUNTAIN REGION

BY JIM KNOPF

Johnson Books: Boulder

To gardeners interested in pioneering a more attractive,
more sustainable Rocky Mountain horticulture.

© 1991 by James M. Knopf

6 7 8 9

Cover and text design by Robert Schram
Photographs by the author except where noted
Drawings by the author

Cover photograph:
These flowers are thriving in low watering zone conditions in
sandy soil, and include Yellow Bearded Iris *(Iris spp.)*, Rocky
Mountain Penstemon *(Penstemon strictus)*, Wild White
Snapdragon *(P. grandiflorus 'Albus')*, Scarlet Bugler Penstemon
(P. barbatus), Pine-leaf Penstemon *(P. pinifolius)*, and Scarlet
Globemallow *(Sphaeralcea coccinea)*.

Library of Congress Cataloging-in-Publication Data
Knopf, Jim.
      The xeriscape flower gardener : a waterwise guide for the Rocky
Mountain region / by Jim Knopf. — 1st ed.
         p.   cm.
      Includes bibliographical references and index.
      ISBN 1-55566-077-0
      1. Xeriscaping — Rocky Mountains Region. 2. Flower gardening —
Rocky Mountains Region   I. Title.
SB475.83.K57   1991
716'.0978—dc20   91-2955
                                                          CIP

Printed in the United States of America by
Johnson Publishing Company
1880 South 57th Court
Boulder, Colorado 80301

THE XERISCAPE
FLOWER &GARDENER

CONTENTS

ACKNOWLEDGMENTS

So many people have generously offered help with this book that there is no way to acknowledge all of them by name. The following people, however, deserve special thanks and recognition: Ken Ball for writing the foreword to this book, as well as for pioneering the concept of Xeriscape with such insight, enthusiasm, and persistence; Panayoti Kelaidis for his timely and extraordinarily skillful review of the manuscript for proper botanic names, and also for pursuing the concept of Tethyan gardening and its application in the Rocky Mountain region; Ellyn Axelrod for her timely and perceptive review of the manuscript, especially the parts related to water rates and utility billing; Lauren Springer for sharing her extensive knowledge of garden plants and plant names; Ray Daugherty for contributing from his impressive familiarity of plants, especially propagation of plants well-adapted to the Rocky Mountain region; Judith Phillips for help in understanding the southern boundary of the Rocky Mountain region; and finally Steve Jones, Nancy Dawson, and my parents for support and advice when it mattered most.

FOREWORD

Many people, cities, and businesses were actively supporting concepts of water-efficient landscaping long before the term "Xeriscape" (pronounced ZIR-i-scape) entered into our vocabulary. Indeed, their efforts and ideas set the stage for Xeriscape, and to a great extent have made it the success it is today.

In 1981, the president of the Associated Landscape Contractors of Colorado, Jim Grabow, proposed to the Denver Water Department that a task force be created for public participation in making landscape water use more efficient. During the course of discussions, Ms. Nancy Leavitt, an environmental planner for the Denver Water Department, coined the term "Xeriscape" from *xeri* (referring to dry), and *scape* (referring to vista). In spite of the derivation, the idea was never intended to focus only on non-irrigated (dry) landscaping, but rather to focus on how to landscape appropriately in dry regions—as a means to conserve water. Therefore, the definition, "water conservation through creative landscaping," was developed.

Since that time, the term has become the common identity for landscape water conservation programs in many parts of the country, with the National Xeriscape Council, Inc. (a non-profit organization) created to encourage international interest, participation, and support for landscape water conservation. A trademark on both the term "Xeriscape" and the logo is held by this organization. In the years that followed the 1982 introduction of the program in Denver, it became clear that the seven Xeriscape fundamentals, promoted widely today, were truly universal and applicable in every climate.

The proactive and positive direction of the concept bolstered its popularity, and news of the program spread quickly through such events and activities as "X-rated" (Xeriscape) garden parties; Xeriscape garden clubs; newspaper, magazine, and television coverage; and educational seminars.

By 1984, the concept had spread through California, Texas, Arizona, and Nevada, and the continued growth in popularity led to the creation of a National Xeriscape Council in 1986. In early 1990, there were active Xeriscape education programs in more than sixty cities in forty-two states, and three foreign countries. Until now, however, there has been a significant shortage of books about Xeriscape—especially books, like this one, about regional Xeriscape horticulture and design.

Xeriscape presents opportunities for everyone—opportunities to live in harmony and balance with our environment, rather than attempting to dominate it in every way; to improve the diversity and interest in community aesthetics; to reduce our water use by 60 percent or more; to reduce soil, water, and air pollution; to protect public properties (including avoiding expensive street repairs caused by overwatering roadside landscaping); opportunities for businesses to grow; and opportunities for species survival, including *Homo sapiens*.

Congratulations for selecting this book, and congratulations for continuing to support water conservation.

Ken Ball
Water Conservation Officer
Denver Water Department

1.

XERISCAPE
&
WATERWISE
FLOWER
GARDENING

The Xeriscape (ZIR-i-scape) approach to landscaping is truly a good news story. As Doug Welsh, president of the National Xeriscape Council, states, "Xeriscape is an opportunity to take a proactive stance and exhibit a true stewardship approach to the most precious of natural resources. It is a 'win-win' situation. Everyone wins: the water agency does its job of efficiently using its resources; the landscape professionals help to bring beauty to the community and ensure their livelihood; the gardener gets a quality landscape that requires less water, less maintenance, and ultimately less dollars; and the educator receives satisfaction by being a facilitator in the entire orchestration of Xeriscape programs." ■

Waterwise Landscaping Makes Sense

 The Xeriscape, or water-efficient, approach to landscaping offers so many outstanding benefits over traditional highly watered landscaping that it is surprising it hasn't already emerged as the most common form of landscape design. The extraordinary savings in water alone are so significant, both to individual property owners and to municipalities trying to keep up with rapidly increasing water-demand, that waterwise landscaping is commanding increasing consideration as a relevant part of water supply planning. In addition, the potential savings in initial landscape construction, as well as in ongoing maintenance, is substantial. All this, together with wonderful new opportunities for year-round, eye-appealing designs, and major business opportunities (both based on increased use of flowers, shrubs, groundcovers, and new types of turfgrasses) makes water-efficient landscaping an increasingly exciting subject.

XERISCAPE FUNDAMENTALS

The seven Xeriscape fundamentals provide a quick idea of how water-efficient landscaping is able to provide so many advantages over traditional landscaping.

1. **Plan and design** comprehensively from the beginning.
2. **Create practical turf areas** of manageable sizes, shapes, and appropriate grasses.
3. **Use appropriate plants and zone the landscape** according to the water needs of the plants.
4. **Consider improving the soil** with organic matter like compost or manure.
5. **Consider using mulches,** such as wood chips.
6. **Irrigate efficiently** with properly designed systems (including hose-end equipment) and by applying the right amount of water at the right time.
7. **Maintain the landscape appropriately** by mowing, pruning, and fertilizing properly.

ECONOMIC BENEFITS

The most common reason for considering Xeriscape as an approach to landscape design is the water savings potential it offers. The magnitude of these savings, however, is not always appreciated, and this becomes clearer when considering that 40 to 60 percent of the drinking water supplied to cities throughout the Rocky Mountain region is being used for landscape irrigation. It becomes still clearer when noting that well-done Xeriscape designs typically reduce irrigation by more than 50 percent, compared with the water used on traditional designs that are frequently dominated by overly watered lawns.

The economic cost of supplying water in unlimited amounts (largely to water Kentucky Bluegrass lawns) is getting prohibitively high in the West. This is illustrated by the gigantic Two Forks project in Colorado, and by the water conservation plan being considered by Boulder, Colorado, to reduce need for expensive expansion of its water treatment capacity (see related story, "The Easy Water Projects Have Already Been Built"). The cost of such massive projects is reflected more and more frequently in increasing local water rates. The upper end of these local rates is illustrated in Santa Fe, New Mexico, and in Lafayette, Colorado, where two ordinary garden hoses (running at full pressure and using about fourteen gallons of water per minute) would cost about $2.90 and $6.88 per hour, respectively, when customers have used enough water to reach the highest rate categories. Sandy and Park City, Utah, are also reported to have very high water rates, but Ocean Reef, Florida, has experienced the highest rates known to date—1¢ per gallon. At this rate, two ordinary garden hoses, running at full pressure of 60 psi, would result in using water at the rate of $8.40 per hour!

There are also significant potential economic savings during initial landscape construction, if less expensive plant species and smaller sizes are selected, and if spacing between plants is increased. Still further savings are possible with many well-done residential designs because they can often be irrigated entirely with inexpensive hose-end equipment.

One study involving two different Xeriscape designs and one traditional lawn-dominated design of the same property resulted in construction cost estimates of $.93/square foot and $1.09/square foot for the Xeriscape designs, and $1.14/square foot for the traditional design. This is explained in more detail in Chapter 2.

Ongoing maintenance costs are more difficult to document precisely, but by creating designs that need less overall maintenance time, and which offer greater flexibility as to when the maintenance must be performed, costs can be reduced substantially. There is more about this in Chapter 4.

Real estate values are also affected greatly by the appearance of the landscape. Landscapes that are more easily maintained, and that offer more flexibility as to when maintenance must be done, tend to be more attractive, more often. In areas affected by periodic severe watering restrictions, the benefits of landscapes that can get by temporarily on reduced irrigation, or even without irrigation, become even more important. During "buyer's markets," it can become important to have a front yard that is not too similar to all the others on the market, and Xeriscape designs offer more opportunity to be different, attractively, than landscapes that are almost entirely lawn.

The "green" industry (sod growers, landscape maintenance companies, nurseries, landscape contractors, garden centers, designers, and so on) all stand to benefit from the diversification in landscaping offered by water-efficient designs.

New varieties of Turf-type Tall Fescue and Buffalograss offer especially dramatic opportunities for enterprising sod growers. Significant increases in business are possible just through marketing the advantages of converting old, water-intensive Kentucky Bluegrass lawns to less water-intensive Turf-type Tall Fescue varieties. Major business opportunities also exist in knowledgeable retail sales, innovative landscape design, landscape maintenance, and irrigation systems. Increasing interest in water-efficient landscaping can realistically be viewed as a practical business opportunity rather than a threat.

ENVIRONMENTAL BENEFITS

A general increasing concern about environmental issues is causing many people to rethink the way we use all natural resources, and this often raises concerns about hardship, sacrifice, and a lower quality of life. Water-conserving landscaping, however, offers a very real way to reduce negative environmental impacts while actually improving the quality of life.

The dramatic water savings available through Xeriscape designs have environmental implications at least equal to the economic benefits previously discussed. The size and number of storage dams is an issue, by itself, with enormous negative consequences for wildlife and plant life throughout the Rocky Mountain region. The transmountain diversions, and collection systems needed for these storage systems, create additional major impacts on wildlife and on human recreation throughout the Rocky Mountain West. The diversion of such massive amounts of water also negatively affects water quality in many areas, and when farm irrigation water is appropriated for urban landscape use, major areas of farming are permanently lost. In some areas, such as Santa Fe, New Mexico, pumping large amounts of water results in another major economic and environmental cost of the water supply.

In a time of increasing awareness of limited resources, the rationality of investing so much in planting, fertilizing, mowing, and harvesting a "crop" (lawn grass) that we usually throw away is questionable at best, especially with so many good alternatives.

Extensive use of plants (like Kentucky Bluegrass) that often require widespread use of herbicides, pesticides, and fertilizers (when grown on inappropriate sites) causes significant problems that can be avoided by using plants more naturally suited to each site. In actuality, Kentucky Bluegrass requires far less fertilizer, herbicides, and pesticides than are typically applied, so on athletic fields and playgrounds, where this grass is appropriate, relatively benign horticultural practices are available.

The practical advantages of the Xeriscape approach to landscaping clearly make it possible for everyone to do something about many of the environmental problems we face.

"The Easy Water Projects Have Already Been Built"

The giant Two Forks water project on the Platte River west of Denver, Colorado, illustrates the extensive problems associated with trying to supply unlimited amounts of water, largely to continue soaking Kentucky Bluegrass lawns.

According to Dan Luecke of the Environmental Defense Fund, the economic costs of this project (the largest nonfederal water project in the West) would likely reach $1 billion, and environmental costs would include flooding the scenic Platte River Canyon, a popular recreation area west of Denver and one of the world's premier trout streams. Downstream, in Nebraska, reduced flow in the Platte River would destroy critical habitat for sandhill and whooping cranes, and diversion of water from west of the Continental Divide would significantly decrease both the quality and quantity of water in the Colorado River. There has also been concern that supplying water to the huge Two Forks Reservoir would eventually lead to major construction in the popular Eagle's Nest Wilderness Area.

To invest up to $1 billion in a massive water project, rather than in parks, schools, fire departments, and other essential urban services (primarily in order to continue unlimited abusive lawn watering) is questionable when landscape irrigation consumes 40 to 60 percent of our drinking water, and water-efficient landscaping has been shown to reduce landscape irrigation water use by more than 50 percent.

A different aspect of water supply expansion problems is clearly illustrated in Boulder, Colorado, where there is adequate water to satisfy a population much larger than Boulder ever expects, but where current water treatment capacity is nearly inadequate to meet landscape irrigation demand on a few blistering days (or even hours) each year.

The Boulder Utilities Division estimates that treatment plant expansion would require a 14 to 16 percent increase in utility rates, while investing in a voluntary water conservation plan (primarily focusing on landscape irrigation to reduce peak demand) would require only a 3 to 4 percent increase in utility rates. With 40 to 60 percent of the drinking water throughout the Rocky Mountain states being used for landscape irrigation, and with local water supply systems throughout the region reaching their logical limits, water conservation—especially landscape water conservation—is very timely. ∎

VISUAL BENEFITS

The eye-appealing visual impact of appropriately used flowers, groundcovers and shrubs, together with appropriate use of traditional and new types of turf, offer exciting opportunities to increase the year-round visual interest of urban and suburban landscapes. There is also an excellent opportunity to create delightful regional landscapes, rather than the generally "look-alike" style that is currently common throughout the United States. In this regard, Santa Fe, New Mexico, offers a truly outstanding model of urban landscaping that makes the most of its natural setting. Taos, New Mexico (similar to Santa Fe), Tucson, Arizona (outside the Rocky Mountain region as defined in this book), and the Genesee area west of Denver offer additional examples of using the local natural landscape with wonderful results.

The Xeriscape fundamental of zoning landscapes (in order to group plants of similar water requirements) creates many wonderful visual opportunities that appeal to increasing numbers of gardeners, and also creates numerous possibilities to enhance urban wildlife habitat. Chapter 6 explores the world of Xeriscape wildlife gardening, and offers many "tricks" for managing wildlife conflicts. The opportunity to develop meaningful links with the rich and rewarding natural heritage of the Rocky Mountain region is almost reason enough to learn as much as possible about the Xeriscape approach to landscape design.

THE CHALLENGE OF XERISCAPE

In spite of the numerous inherent advantages of Xeriscape, one of the reasons it is not yet a widespread approach to landscaping is that water-efficient designs so often appear too lush and colorful to be recognized as saving extraordinary amounts of water, while cactus and gravel gardens, on the other hand, immediately appear to be saving water. Ironically, cactus and gravel gardens may actually be increasing the water demand of nearby plants, by raising the temperature—ZEROscape is a good term for this.

Because good, water-efficient designs are frequently not immediately self-evident, there is a need to see what they look like in various ordinary landscape situations. To be as helpful as possible in addressing this need to visualize well-done waterwise landscaping, as well as to provide practical advice about creating and maintaining Xeriscape designs, this book focuses on just one horticultural region—the Rocky Mountain region—and on waterwise flower gardening, perhaps the least understood aspect of Rocky Mountain horticulture.

As Doug Welsh, president of the National Xeriscape Council in 1990, has pointed out, plants don't waste water—people do, and people can learn to change their attitudes and habits in order to reduce water waste. This may require a little pioneering spirit, as well as a little experimenting and perseverance, but the economic, environmental, visual, and psychological rewards are well worth the effort. Xeriscape is a truly good news story.

The Rocky Mountain Region

Mind-boggling variability, unpredictability, and extremes characterize the weather across the Rocky Mountain region of North America. This is a land where "abnormal is normal, and normal is abnormal," where "weather forecasts are the epitome of irrelevance," and where local residents recognize that "only fools, foreigners, and television weatherjesters try to forecast the weather."

Many common garden problems in the Rocky Mountain region arise because much of the horticultural information available to gardeners in this area is based on experience elsewhere, and often seriously underestimates the advantages, as well as the disadvantages, of the rigorous Rocky Mountain climate.

For one thing, the effect of very low humidity is rarely considered in many gardening books from other regions, and low humidity is a major factor in this region, especially when compounded by the intense sunshine and high summer temperatures common throughout the region. A temperature of 95°F with 95 percent humidity, for example, is very different from 95°F with 5 percent humidity. Among other things, this makes annual precipitation comparisons with wetter regions almost meaningless.

The effect of prevailing low humidity is illustrated clearly in Boulder, Colorado, where a rain barrel filled with 37 inches of water on the first of January would gain about 18 inches of water from average rain and snow, but would be empty by the end of the year. Average weather would evaporate 55 inches of water! Variability in the weather is also worth noting. Natural precipitation in Boulder has varied from a high of 29.09 inches to a low of 10.91 inches, with similar variations in evaporation rates.

The abundance and intensity of sunlight are additional significant factors to consider. Not only are there more hours of sunlight in much of the Rocky Mountain region, compared with cloudier places, but the intensity of the sunlight is also greater. For example, ultraviolet light (just one measure of the strength of sunlight) increases approximately 50 to 60 percent between sea level and 6,000 feet at 40° latitude north. This means that many plants (such as rhubarb and strawberries) that require full sun in other regions will grow well in partial shade in the Rocky Mountain region.

Microclimates (localized differences in prevailing weather conditions) are another misunderstood factor that can lead to trouble in Rocky Mountain gardening. Although microclimates are often cursed, they are actually one of the real assets of gardening in this region, because they allow more kinds of plants to be grown in the space of a single yard than is possible in regions where the microclimates are less differentiated.

This can be illustrated by considering the differences between the north and south sides of a typical suburban house in the Rocky Mountain region. Sunlight, air temperature, and humidity against the south wall will fluctuate wildly. Sixty- to seventy-degree Fahrenheit temperature changes in a few hours (or even a few minutes) are not uncommon. This allows desert gardens to flourish against south walls, while near a north wall of the same house, aspen and columbine from the mountains may thrive without irrigation. The shadow areas near north-facing and east-facing walls are perhaps the only places where roof runoff water can be used effectively. In these areas, runoff is likely to be available long enough to satisfy many plants. In contrast, roof runoff water used in sunny areas, near south-facing and west-facing walls, usually evaporates too quickly to be helpful. In cloudy and cold periods in the same locations, runoff water may last long enough to be a problem for plants that need well-drained soil. It is not exaggeration to say that these differences in one yard can represent several thousand feet of elevation change in the mountains, or several thousand miles of latitude change on the plains. Ignoring these differences creates real frustration, while consciously adapting to them will work wonders.

Trying to determine plant hardiness by using information based on other regions is one of the most troublesome problems for plant pioneers in the Rocky Mountain region. The U.S. Department of Agriculture (USDA) plant hardiness classification system (based on average minimum winter temperature), for example, is almost useless in estimating plant success in this region. In and near the Rocky Mountains, drastic temperature fluctuations in spring and fall are much more likely to determine success or failure with plants than average minimum winter temperature.

Problems with the USDA system are illustrated by gardeners in the mountainous portions of the region, who frequently discover that it is the lack of summer heat, rather than minimum winter temperature, that limits the use of many plants that are very successful at lower elevations. For example, the use of Piñon Pine at ski resort areas is sometimes unsuccessful due to lack of summer heat, rather than low minimum winter temperature. Likewise, gardeners in Denver may find that heat-loving plants (such as

Blackfoot Daisy) will do well only in sunny, hot spots, even though nighttime winter temperatures are the same elsewhere in the same garden. Defining plant hardiness is generally much more complex in the West than in the East, but it is also much more interesting, because there are so many more factors to consider.

Across the Rocky Mountain region, there are some notable differences in the local climate to be considered, but the combination of prevailing temperature, precipitation, sunlight, soil types, and other factors create a generally similar set of horticultural conditions. The greatest of these local climate differences are based first on differences in elevation, and second on differences in latitude. A third major factor is the effect of mountain ranges on the movement of cold fronts and storms through the region.

The following formula is useful in estimating the differences in climate that are related to altitude and latitude:

> 100 feet higher = 1 day later in the spring, and 1 day earlier in the fall.
>
> 100 feet lower = 1 day earlier in the spring, and 1 day later in the fall.
>
> 1 degree of latitude = 70 statute miles = 300 feet higher or lower = 3 days.

Because this formula is based on temperature changes (typically about 3.5° to 5.5°F per thousand feet of elevation change), this formula works best in the spring, because spring leaf and flower development is almost entirely dependent on temperature, while fall color change is dependent on shortening day length, in combination with temperature and available moisture.

A comparison between Santa Fe, New Mexico, and Denver, Colorado, illustrates the different effects of altitude, latitude, and mountains. According to the formula, Santa Fe, which is about three hundred miles south of Denver, but about two thousand feet higher, would be a little colder than Denver. Comparing weather records, however, will show that *average* temperatures are very similar in the two cities, but that Denver is more likely to be either much warmer or colder than its average temperature much of the time. A close observation of plants growing in Santa Fe indicates that the climate must actually be somewhat milder than Denver. Evergreen Photinia (*Photinia spp.*), for example, grows in Santa Fe, but not in Denver, and Atlas Cedar (*Cedrus atlantica*) seems to grow without winter injury in Santa Fe, while the few Atlas Cedar survivors in the Denver area usually show signs of significant winter injury. The explanation of these differences

CLIMATE DATA FOR ROCKY MOUNTAIN CITIES

City	Alt.	Lat.	Jan. Temp.°F H	L	Noon Hum.	Poss. Sun	Rain Snow	July Temp.°F H	L	Noon Hum.	Poss. Sun	Rain Snow	Rec. Temp.°F H	L	Annual Precp.	Frost-free Season
Denver, CO	5280	39°30'N	42°	15°	43%	73%	.55"	88°	57°	36%	72%	1.53"	105°	-30°	14.8"	159 Days (6 May–12 Oct)
Reno, NV	4397	39°30'N	46°	17°	54%	65%	1.04"	92°	47°	19%	91%	.23"	106°	-19°	6.96"	141 Days (14 May–2 Oct)
S.L. City, UT	4220	40°46'N	36°	17°	70%	46%	1.20"	92°	61°	23%	82%	.61"	106°	-30°	14.74"	202 Days (12 Apr–1 Nov)
Santa Fe, NM	7200	35°40'N	41°	19°	54%	70%	.52"	85°	62°	33%	78%	1.84"	109°	-24°	11.88"	165 Days (3 May–15 Oct)
Albuquerque, NM	5311	35°03'N	46°	24°	36%	73%	.41"	91°	66°	28%	76%	1.20"	104°	-17°	8.13"	196 Days (16 Apr–29 Oct)
Spokane, WA	2357	47°37'N	31°	19°	74%	28%	2.40"	86°	55°	23%	82%	.38"	108°	-30°	17.19"	169 Days (25 Apr–11 Oct)
Flagstaff, AZ	6993	35°08'N	40°	14°	51%	—	1.83"	81°	50°	33%	90%	2.28"	97°	-30°	18.3"	110 Days (8 Jun–26 Sep)
Boise, ID	2838	43°54'N	36°	22°	72%	39%	1.64"	91°	59°	22%	87%	.26"	112°	-23°	11.43"	159 Days (6 May–12 Oct)
Rapid City, SD	3165	44°02'N	33°	9°	61%	55%	.48"	86°	59°	40%	73%	2.06"	110°	-33°	17.1"	150 Days (7 May–4 Oct)
Pierre, SD	1719	44°23'N	28°	7°	—	—	.44"	91°	63°	—	—	1.72"	108°	-20°	16.5"	—
Bismarck, ND	1650	46°46'N	20°	-2°	71%	54%	.36"	86°	59°	49%	75%	2.33"	109°	-44°	15.4"	136 Days (11 May–24 Sep)
Sheridan, WY	3942	44°46'N	33°	7°	62%	57%	.75"	86°	55°	35%	76%	1.38"	106°	-31°	16.8"	123 Days (21 May–21 Oct)
Dodge City, KS	2594	37°46'N	42°	19°	58%	68%	.49"	93°	67°	42%	78%	2.63"	109°	-26°	20.6"	184 Days (22 Apr–24 Oct)
N. Platte, NE	2779	41°08'N	37°	11°	63%	54%	.39"	89°	62°	42%	76%	2.40"	112°	-35°	17.5"	160 Days (30 Apr–7 Oct)
Great Falls, MT	3662	47°29'N	32°	13°	63%	51%	.61"	85°	54°	29%	81%	1.28"	106°	-43°	14"	135 Days (14 May–26 Oct)
Billings, MT	3567	45°48'N	33°	13°	57%	50%	.54"	89°	61°	31%	79%	.90"	112°	-49°	13.2"	132 Days (15 May–24 Oct)
Amarillo, TX	3604	35°14'N	50°	24°	42%	70%	.65"	94°	67°	38%	77%	2.34"	108°	+16°	19.7"	191 Days (20 Apr–28 Oct)
Wichita, KS	1321	37°39'N	40°	19°	63%	58%	.68"	93°	70°	48%	75%	3.62"	114°	-22°	28.6"	186 Days (16 Apr–19 Oct)
Lethbridge, Alb.	3017	49°58'N	27°	9°	71%	39%	—	78°	52°	39%	71%	.84"	102°	-45°	17"	125+ Days (NA)
Indianapolis, IN	793	39°44'N	37°	21°	72%	36%	3.15"	88°	64°	54%	74%	3.03"	106°	-25°	40"	186 Days (16 Apr–19 Oct)

Sources:

1. Lance Walheim & Robert Stebbins, *Western Fruit Berries & Nuts*, HP Books, Tucson, Arizona, 1981.
2. Richard Keen, *Skywatch*, Fulcrum, Inc., Golden, Colorado, 1987.
3. *1989 Weather Guide Calendar*, Accord Publishing, Ltd., Denver, Colorado.
4. *Tables of Temperature, Relative Humidity, Precipitation, and Sunshine for the World*, Her Majesty's Stationery Office, London, 1983.
5. Hare & Thomas, *Climate Canada*, Wiley Publishers of Canada, Ltd., Toronto, 1974.
6. *Climate of the States*, NOAA, & Gale Research Co., 1985.
7. *Climate of the States*, NOAA, & Gale Research Co., 1987.

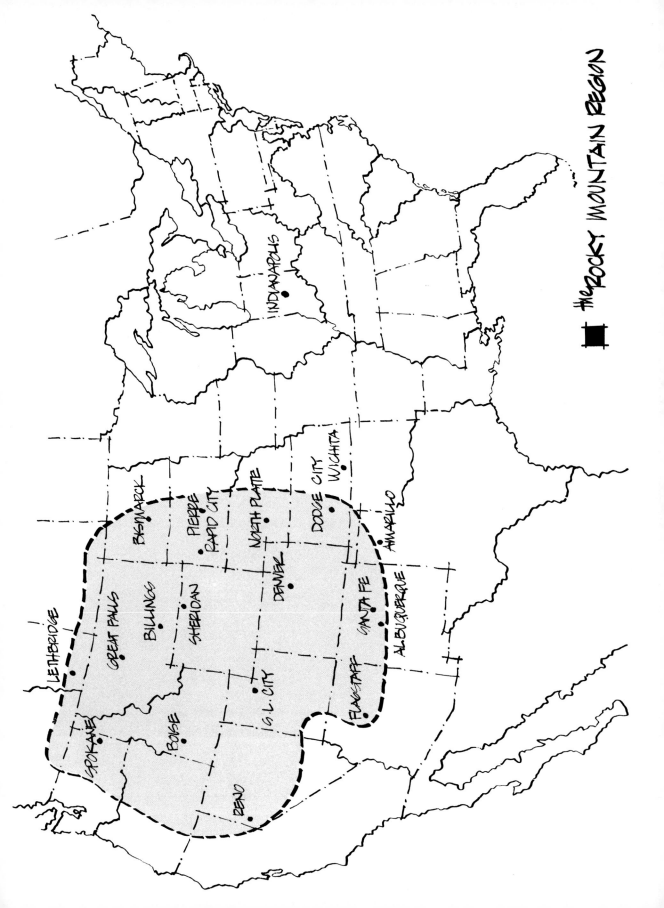

the ROCKY MOUNTAIN REGION

may lie in the relative location of the nearby mountains. Denver is located east of the mountains, and thus is exposed to the full force of continental arctic air masses, while Santa Fe's position west of the Sangre de Cristo mountains protects it from many of the same arctic cold fronts. In addition, Denver is east of a very high portion of the nearby continental divide, making it vulnerable to dramatic warming downslope (chinook) winds. The resulting drastic rising and falling winter temperatures very likely add considerable extra stress to plants, and may help explain some of the differences in the plants that grow well in these two locations.

Across the Rocky Mountain region, differences like those between Santa Fe and Denver are interesting, but a range of similar features nevertheless characterize these areas as a general horticultural region.

The chart on page 10 illustrates more of the climatic differences and similarities within the Rocky Mountain region. Indianapolis (in the center of the Midwest) is included for comparison. Albuquerque is located in an area of transition to the desert southwest, but is similar enough that much of the information in this book will still be useful. In Albuquerque, increasing the watering recommendations by as much as 25 percent might be necessary, but plants within each watering zone would still be the same. A fourth zone might be added for plants that will thrive with no irrigation in Albuquerque. Amarillo, Texas, and Wichita, Kansas, are probably best placed outside the region, but still have enough in common with the region that much of the information will be useful.

Advantages of Waterwise Flower Gardening

The abundant, intense sunlight, low humidity, warm days with cool nights, and low natural precipitation in the Rocky Mountain region combine to create some of the showiest floral displays anywhere. When it comes to annual, biennial, and perennial flowers, the Rocky Mountain region is second to none. The expression "floral fireworks" may not be an exaggeration.

Potential low-maintenance (or practicality) is another good reason to consider using flowers more often in Rocky Mountain landscaping, whether residential, commercial, or public. Arid and semiarid flower gardens can be considered especially low-maintenance when compared with wet gardens and Kentucky Bluegrass "lawnscaping." To put it simply, flowers can wait, while heavily watered lawns require very regular mowing, trimming, and fertilizing. Because flowers don't show neglect immediately, and sometimes look best if not overly managed, it could be said that flower gardens will even wait gracefully until the weather, the gardener's schedule, and the mood synchronize. Waiting, even to the point of "benign neglect," sometimes works small wonders in the garden. "Freebee" or "volunteer" seedlings, for example, can make it possible to have enough difficult-to-buy plants, like Grecian Foxglove (*Digitalis lanata*), to give away to friends. It's amazing how often "volunteer" seedlings come up in great places.

Weeding isn't the problem people often think it will be either—especially with arid and semiarid flower gardens. The prevailing dry surface conditions in these gardens limit most weed seed germination to a brief "weed season" in the spring.

Although overall time-per-square-foot spent maintaining dry flower gardens can be considerably less than that spent maintaining similar areas of Kentucky Bluegrass, time is not the only consideration. Partly because flower gardens are frequently not very familiar, while lawns are very familiar, a significant number of gardeners seem to accept the notion of mowing half a day, once a week, more readily than the idea of bending down to pull even one weed. Psychology, rather than practicality, is clearly part of the decision about landscaping styles.

The most important point is that *landscapes can be tailored to increase the things that gardeners like to do, while reducing those things they don't like to do.*

Waterwise Watering Zones

It is worthwhile to take the time to define watering zones carefully, because they represent one of the most water conserving of the seven Xeriscape fundamentals. The following three zones (developed in Denver, Colorado) can serve as a useful guide. The amount of water indicated in *inches per week* refers to typical Denver midsummer irrigation needs for periods without rain. The figures in *gallons per square feet* refer to irrigation needed for a typical 20-week irrigation season.

High Watering Zones:	Moderate Watering Zones:	Low Watering Zones:
■ 18-20 gals. added per sq. ft. per 20-week season	■ 10± gals. added per sq. ft. per 20-week season	■ 0 to 3 gals. added per sq. ft. per 20-week season
■ .5″ added 3 times per week	■ .75″ added once per week	■ .5″ added every other week
■ Approx. 30″ added over 20 wks.	■ Approx. 16″ added over 20 wks.	■ Approx. 4.5″ added over 20 wks.
Typical plants: Kentucky Bluegrass lawns, Redtwig Dogwood, Pansies	*Typical plants: Turf-type Tall Fescue lawns, Potentilla, Purple Coneflower*	*Typical plants: Buffalograss lawns, Rabbitbrush, Mexican Hat Coneflower*

- Every site will have unique combinations of soil, sun, slopes, and so on. This will require adjustments to the amounts of water needed in each zone. Sandy soil, for example, typically requires more water than clay soils, and south-facing or west-facing slopes typically require surprisingly more water than level areas.
- At altitudes higher than the Denver area, or in areas with hotter and drier summers, additional adjustments will be called for. Throughout the Rocky Mountain West, plants that are well suited to each zone should remain the same.
- It is important to note that many plants will grow well in more than one zone.
- *It is also important to avoid adjacent high and low watering zones whenever possible.* High watering zones adjacent to sunny sidewalks, for example, inevitably lead to the waste of considerable water on the pavement, while placing high watering zones adjacent to low-water plantings usually encourages weeds at the edge of the xeric zones, where too much water is almost always applied by sprinklers overshooting their zones.

Terms & Concepts

Because the following terms and concepts are used in so many different ways, they are defined here to clarify how they are used in this book.

Native plant: This is a particularly troublesome term, and even dictionary definitions of the term vary considerably. In the strictest sense, this term refers to plants that originate in a particular place. However, this does not entirely eliminate the possibility of introduction at some much earlier time. *Endemic* is often considered synonymous, but it goes beyond this definition of native plant by eliminating the idea of previous introduction. *Indigenous* is also frequently considered synonymous, but this term, strictly speaking, emphasizes limited distribution of a plant.

To help avoid additional confusion, waterwise gardeners might want to consider the following information about native plants:
- Even though plants are often considered native to political units such as Arizona, the United States, or China, plants evolve in ecological territories, not political units. This is illustrated close to home, where Shrubby Potentilla (*Potentilla fruticosa*) is often considered a native plant in Denver. However, it is not native in Denver. It is native to the mountains of Colorado instead. Strictly speaking, it would be more appropriately considered native in parts of Tibet, China, and Scandinavia, before considering it native in Denver.
- There are also several biases and assumptions about native plants that can cause problems. One of these involves all-too-common comments that plants native to dry regions must be well adapted to dry gardens. This overlooks plants such as Cattails

(*Typha spp.*), Cottonwoods (*Populus spp.*), and Redtwig Dogwood (*Cornus stolonifera*) that are native to wet places in dry regions. It is also common to encounter comments that native plants must be more disease and insect resistant than introduced plants. Again, this fails to recognize that plants such as native Box Elder (*Acer negundo*) and Common Hackberry (*Celtis occidentalis*) are hosts to many insects, while introduced Russian Olive (*Elaeagnus angustifolia*) is almost insect-free.

While it is both interesting and useful to recognize and respect plants that are original members of a local ecosystem, it is also important to recognize that plants introduced from other ecosystems can be very appropriate in responsible gardening. It is also useful and appropriate to consider natural varieties that are more drought tolerant, more colorful, or more disease resistant than standard varieties. Plants of artificial hybrid origin, however, are likely to be better adapted to artificial cultivation than to natural conditions.

Introduced plant: This is usually a reference to plants that have been introduced from some other natural setting, but the term does not exclude plants of human hybrid origin. *Exotic plant* is a term that is often used synonymously, but it can also refer to plants that are unfamiliar, odd, or strikingly unusual.

Naturalized plant: This term refers to plants that have adapted enough to a new environment that they reproduce to some degree in the new surroundings.

Wildflower: A wildflower is simply a flowering plant that grows in a natural, uncultivated situation. It is not necessarily native, and a wildflower may or may not reproduce indefinitely on a specific site. The word wildflower is used for so many different concepts that it is important to consider, consciously, what is intended each time it is used.

Weed: Several definitions illustrate the wide range of possible meanings of this word. For example, "A plant with a greater will to live," "A plant you haven't learned to love—yet," "A plant in the wrong place," "A plant with noxious qualities."

Designer weed: This is a light-hearted reference to common "weeds" worth a second look, because they are very durable and have significant ornamental value. Given new names, and a little capitalistic advertising hype, many of these "weeds with potential" can be converted from targets of misguided weed ordinances to coveted money-making items for yuppie gardeners and Xeriscape enthusiasts.

Xeriscape (syn. water-efficient landscaping): This term was coined in 1981 by the Associated Landscape Contractors of

Colorado, and was first used publicly in Denver in 1982. Even though the syllables technically refer to dry and vista, the original intent was to promote conservation of water through water-efficient landscaping. In order to help define the term, and to help promote understanding of how to accomplish truly water-efficient landscaping, the following seven Xeriscape fundamentals have been promoted along with the term Xeriscape. The fundamentals are defined here in accord with the National Xeriscape Council, which holds a trademark on the word Xeriscape, and on the official logo.

1. **Plan and design** comprehensively from the beginning.
2. **Create practical turf areas** of manageable sizes, shapes, and appropriate grasses.
3. **Use appropriate plants and zone the landscape** according to the water needs of the plants.
4. **Consider improving the soil** with organic matter, such as compost or manure.
5. **Consider using mulches,** such as woodchips.
6. **Irrigate efficiently** with properly designed systems (including hose-end equipment) and by applying the right amount of water at the right time.
7. **Maintain the landscape appropriately** by mowing, pruning, and fertilizing properly.

The following misconceptions about "Xeriscape" have significantly hindered the widespread realization of the benefits of well-done, water-efficient landscaping.

Misconception #1: Xeriscape means rocks and yuccas, or cactus and gravel. This is perhaps the most familiar misuse of the term Xeriscape. Ironically rocks and yucca may even increase water use, by raising the temperature around nearby plants. It is also ironic because rock and yucca landscaping is not necessarily lower maintenance than other types of landscaping. *ZEROscape is a good term for rock and yucca landscaping.*

Misconception #2: Xeriscape means no lawns. This is absolutely not true. Well-done Xeriscapes may, in fact, have some highly watered turf, as well as some low or moderately watered turf. Athletic fields and other high-activity areas, for example, are very appropriately landscaped with highly watered turf, because this type of turf repairs itself after heavy use. There are also an increasing number of less water-demanding alternative types of turf, such as the new varieties of Turf-type Tall Fescue, Buffalo-grass, and Blue Grama to consider. *Less lawn landscaping does not mean lawnless landscaping.* Well-considered use of turf is completely consistent with water-efficient landscaping.

Misconception #3: Xeriscape means dry landscaping only. Even though the term technically refers to dry and vista, the intention has always been to focus on water conservation through water-efficient landscaping, and this involves thoughtful use of highly watered areas, as well as moderately and very seldom watered areas. In fact, appropriate irrigation is a very integral part of the concept of Xeriscape.

Waterwise landscaping: This term is synonymous with Xeriscape.

Water-efficient landscaping: This is also synonymous with Xeriscape.

Xeric: A reference to dry conditions, or to adaptations to dry conditions.

Mesic: A reference to moderately moist conditions, or to adaptations to moderately moist conditions.

Semiarid: A reference to climates that are characterized by light and highly variable precipitation. Semiarid is a good description of the climate of much of the Rocky Mountain region, where conditions can be quite dry or quite wet, but where dry conditions typically define the majority of ecosystems.

Drought-tolerant and **xerophytic**: As used in this book, these terms simply refer to plants that are in some way well adapted to dry conditions. Both of these terms are sometimes defined as referring to plants that are truly adapted to dry conditions, as opposed to plants that escape from drought by going dormant or developing roots that reach down to permanent water, for example.

Perennial plant: As used in this book, this term refers to an herbaceous plant that lives for more than two years. *Perennial annual:* this is a light-hearted reference to plants that are technically annuals, but which come back year after year from seeds so persistently that they are almost perennial elements of the garden. *Perannual:* another expression (reportedly used in College Station, Texas) to refer to "perennial annuals."

Short-lived perennial plant: Used in this book to differentiate perennials that are likely to live for only three to five years from those that are likely to be nearly permanent.

Biennial plant: A plant that typically completes its life cycle in two years.

Annual plant: A plant that typically completes its life cycle in one season. However, this term is also applied to plants that must be replanted annually, because they are not winter hardy. *Annual* *perennial:* A light-hearted reference to plants that are regularly referred to as perennials, but which in practice die out annually.

Ephemeral plant: A plant that lasts for a brief time, or which has a life cycle of less than a year.

Meadow: As used in this book, a meadow is simply an attractive mix of grasses and wildflowers. The grasses and wildflowers may or may not be native to the local ecosystem. The word *prairie* is often used synonymously with meadow.

ET Rate: This is an abbreviation of the term evapo-transpiration rate, and refers to water loss due to evaporation and metabolic transpiration of water from plants. ET rates are commonly used as a guideline for landscape irrigation. There are several problems with the use of ET ratings in landscape irrigation, however. These are explained in Chapter 4.

Low maintenance. When used appropriately, this is simply a reference to landscapes that need relatively less maintenance than other types of landscaping. In common conversational use, however, low maintenance is often confused with no maintenance.

Puttering: A term used by gardeners to refer to enjoyable low-key maintenance that can be done when it is pleasant. Kentucky Bluegrass lawns are rarely candidates for maintenance by puttering, while waterwise flower gardens are usually very well maintained by puttering.

Topsoil: This term is commonly used to refer to good garden soil, rather than to soil from the surface. Unfortunately, surface soil may or may not be good garden soil. The principle of "buyer beware" should be followed when buying topsoil. It may be worse than the soil it is intended to improve. *Black dirt* is also a term that is commonly used for good garden soil, but again exercise caution—some "black dirt" is not good garden soil.

Mountain Peat: A reference to soil that primarily consists of decomposed sedge leaves and roots. In practice, this material is highly variable, sometimes containing too much clay, and sometimes being of too high pH for a good soil amendment.

Sphagnum peat moss: A reference to soil that primarily consists of decomposed sphagnum moss (*Sphagnum spp.*). This material is not mined in the Rocky Mountain states and is a very good component of potting soils.

Perlite: A very useful ingredient in potting soil. It is a mineral that is expanded by heating to form light, porous granules.

Plant names: Considerable confusion can arise from the numerous "common" or English language names for the same plant. Unfortunately, the opposite problem arises with many introduced native plants, which have no English language names. Even botanic names can be a problem, because botanists do not always agree on a single botanic name for the same plant. Most of the confusion, however, can be avoided by using both an English language name and a botanic name. In this book, the botanic names used usually come from either *Hortus Third* or *Flora of the Great Plains*. Both of these are widely available, and both cross-reference many plant name synonyms. The English language (or familiar) names come from many sources, in an attempt to use the most universally familiar names within the Rocky Mountain region.

2.

Planning & Designing Waterwise Gardens

In landscapes designed for water efficiency, flowers have compelling advantages over traditional lawns in many situations. Considering the beauty and relative low-maintenance needs of semiarid flowers, they could be appropriately incorporated into landscaping much more often than they have been. Artistically and pragmatically, flowers can be used to equal advantage in private, public, or commercial landscaping, where they can be planted in borders or islands —or make up entire landscapes. ■

Fitting Flowers into Waterwise Landscapes

 Most landscapes have many corners and other awkward places, such as boulders in the middle of lawn areas or planting islands within parking areas, that make watering and trimming lawns difficult. A preferable approach to such problem areas is to plant them with hardy perennial flowers that require far less maintenance.

Along sunny sidewalks, for example (especially if the ground slopes to the south), there is a sort of double jeopardy situation when trying to maintain an evenly watered lawn. First, it is very difficult to water lawn areas that are adjacent to pavement without wasting a lot of water on the pavement. Second, soil adjacent to sun-warmed pavement dries out much faster than in other areas and therefore requires even more water to maintain a uniform green color.

Fortunately, there are many colorful, durable flowers that will thrive in the extra heat and drier conditions along sunny sidewalks. The moderate and low watering zone plant lists in Chapter 7 contain many plants for such situations.

Generally, the sunnier the area, the greater the choice of plants and the greater the color effect will be. In the high-intensity sunlight of the Rocky Mountain region, however, many plants will bloom successfully in partial shade, or even full shade, where they would not perform well in cloudier, wetter regions.

The Site Planning Process

The appropriate, successful use of waterwise flower gardens in the landscape begins with effective overall site planning. Whether contemplating converting an existing water-consuming "lawn-scape" or a cactus-and-gravel ZEROscape to a Xeriscape, or if starting from scratch on an empty site, it is wise and effective to consider the site planning process widely used by design professionals.

The process begins with a scale drawing of the area being planned. Tracing paper overlays are then used to try out different options, in order to avoid unnecessary redrawing of the original site plan. This process is explained and illustrated with drawings and photos of some of the same property that is used in other parts of this book in order to illustrate the value of following a systematic approach to design.

1   **Site inventory and analysis.** This step involves noting important existing conditions in the area. Drainage, sun and shade conditions, good or bad views, soil types, existing plants, and so on, are all noted with analytical comments.

This photo and drawing illustrate a situation in which moderately drought-tolerant flowers (moderate watering zone) offer a very practical alternative to irrigated Kentucky Bluegrass. Flowers shown include Coronation Gold Yarrow (*Achillea* × *'Coronation Gold'*), Scarlet Bugler Penstemon (*Penstemon barbatus*), and Snow-in-summer (*Cerastium tomentosum*). The large flowering shrub is a Mockorange (*Philadelphus spp.*), which thrives in moderate watering zone conditions. One setting of an even-coverage sprinkler would accomplish all necessary watering. The flowers are located in the outer portion of the sprinkler pattern, where less water falls — ideal for moderate and low watering zone flowers. The flowers are also planted on a south-facing slope, a situation that favors heat-loving flowers, but makes cool-season Kentucky Bluegrass difficult to grow well. The highly watered lawn near the street could well be replaced with such low watering zone plants as Buffalograss and junipers.

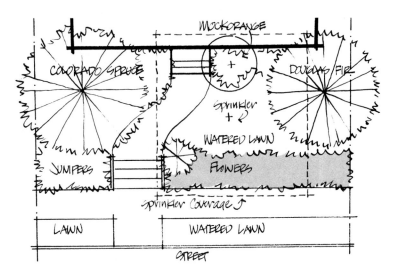

■ SITE INVENTORY-ANALYSIS

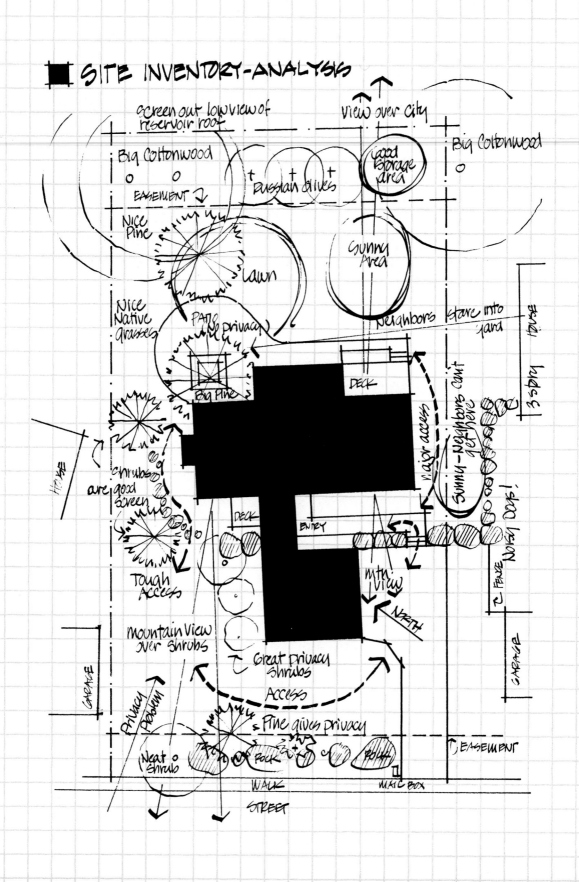

screen out low view of reservoir roof

view over city

Big Cottonwood

Good Storage Area

Big Cottonwood

EASEMENT

Russian olives

Nice Pine

Sunny Area

Nice Native grasses

Lawn

Neighbors stare into yard

PATIO (no privacy)

DECK

Big Pine

Major access

Sunny—Neighbors can't see here

3 story house

Fence

shrubs are good screen

HOUSE

DECK

ENTRY

To fence noisy dogs!

Tough Access

mtn view

NORTH

GARAGE

mountain view over shrubs

Great Privacy Shrubs

Access

GARAGE

Privacy Problem

Pine gives privacy

EASEMENT

Neat shrubs

ROCK

ROCK

WALK

MAIL BOX

STREET

■ DIAGRAMMATIC DESIGN

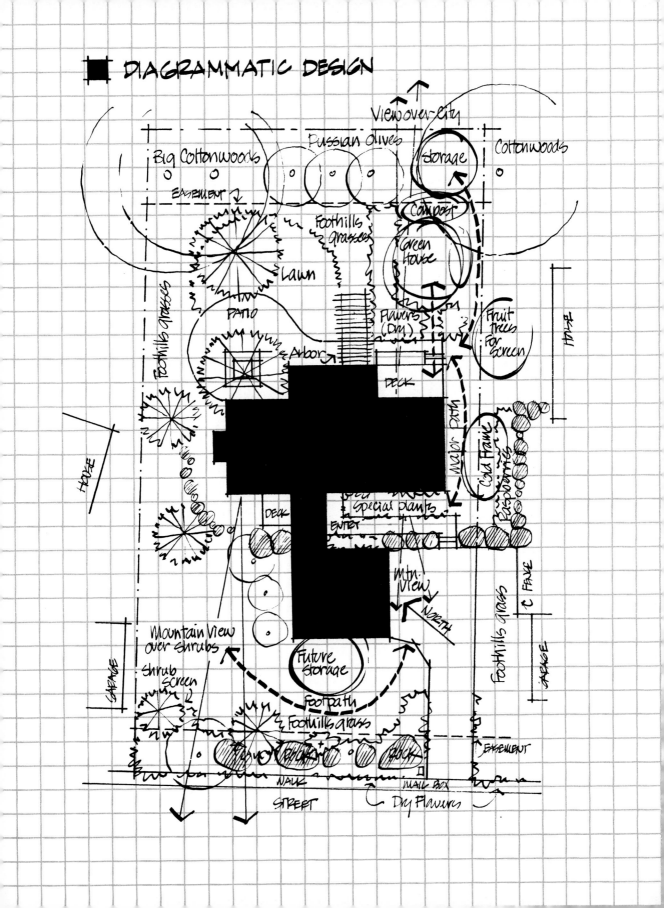

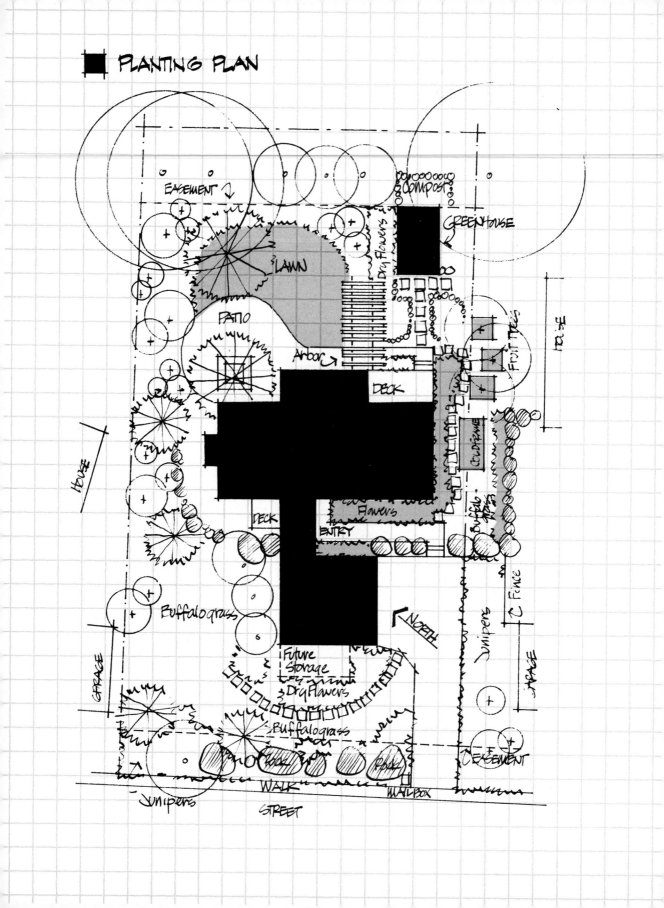

2 **Program development.** This step is a written exercise. It begins by listing desired activities and related facilities that need to be included in the final design. After developing this list, the next stage of program development is to group items from the list according to those that can be accommodated in the same areas of the design and those that must be separated. The final stage of program development is to articulate specific themes that may become part of the final planting design. Attracting or discouraging wildlife, vegetable or flower gardening, very low maintenance, and edible landscaping are examples of themes that are good to identify early in the site planning process.

3 **Diagrammatic design.** The purposes of this step are to consider appropriate locations for various activities identified in the program study, while keeping in mind movement throughout the area being designed (such as auto access, foot traffic, and moving things from front to back yards). This is done by integrating information from the program development and the site inventory and analysis steps, and sketching out alternative plans on tracing paper site overlays.

4 **Planting plans.** The previous steps lead finally to one or more planting plans and provide the means to choose plants with particular purposes in mind. Plants that will screen or frame views, provide edible produce, or encourage butterflies in the garden can all be selected relatively easily at this step.

Going through the site planning process is very useful even if one plans to hire a professional to prepare a formal site plan. Professional designers can work faster and more effectively when clients are able to explain their interests after working through the steps in this process.

Tricks of the Trade for First-time Designers

Sooner or later every designer is faced with the prospect of "kerplunk design," "horrible hodgepodge," or some other cardinal sin of design. But even the most timid first-time designer has reason for hope with the following design tricks. They really work.

Group things and group the groups. Whether working with rocks, flower pots, or a group of shrubs, grouping things and then grouping the groups immediately begins to create order out of chaos and avoids haphazard, "kerplunk" design. After grouping things, *vary the size and vary the space between elements of the groups*. This adds interest to the groups, and makes them look more natural.

Consciously considering these principles works wonders in an amazing array of situations. When beginning a large perennial bed, for example, set out the plants in several groups—starting at a large boulder, perhaps, or at a corner. It suddenly won't matter if there are sufficient plants to fill the entire area. When drawing groups of plants on a planting plan, try using several sizes of circles, and try overlapping some of the circles. Right away it will look better than evenly spaced circles of the same size. Or, try an experiment on the kitchen counter: push a counter-full of typical countertop items into several groups, then vary the spaces between some of the items. This will almost instantly create order out of countertop chaos.

Consciously consider the edges in the design. Where long, unmowed meadow grass meets short, mowed lawn, the trick is to mow to the same line each time; there is no need for dangerous, sharp metal edges. Where lawn meets boulders, try planting Daylilies or Creeping Mahonia (*Mahonia repens*) to create an edge that is easier to maintain. The mower will be able to do all the trimming, and the weed eater can be retired permanently. Carefully considering edges in the design will offer a chance to reduce maintenance and enhance the appearance significantly.

Plan for year-round interest. Twigs, seeds, leaves, and flowers can all be considered in planning for year-round interest in the landscape. The seeds of Rabbitbrush (*Chrysothamnus spp.*), and later the color of the winter stems, for example, are often just as colorful as the more familiar flowers. The curious, ridged twigs of Winged Euonymus (*Euonymus alata*) are very interesting in midwinter and are just as valuable as the earlier flaming red fall color of the plant. A few boulders and shrubs placed in a perennial flower garden can add valuable vertical elements during the winter, when the herbaceous perennials have all died back to ground level. The possibilities are limitless, but it takes some conscious creativity and an ability to pretend it's a cold night in January, when it's really a sweltering day in mid-July.

Color schemes in flower gardens. Trying to create very specific color effects is often not worth the effort. In most cases, it is more satisfying to strive for relatively continuous, multicolor displays from early spring to late fall. Even though fickle spring and fall weather in this region will sometimes wreck long-anticipated dreams of delightful floral displays, they will succeed often enough to be worth the effort.

Color preferences are clearly personal, but several specific combinations have enough universal appeal to be worth mentioning. For example, the spectacular blue flowers of Russian Sage (*Perovskia atriplicifolia*) together with the intriguing wine-red flowers of Poppy Mallow (*Callirhoe involucrata*) frequently draw

rave reviews. Likewise, the combination of the blue flowers of
Pitcher Sage (*Salvia pitcheri*) and the yellow flowers of Rabbitbrush (*Chrysothamnus spp.*) is quite pleasing. Low-growing
Blackfoot Daisy (*Melampodium leucanthum*) is a conspicuous
complement to plants of almost any color.

Sketching from slides. This is an almost foolproof way to try
out ideas without having to construct elaborate architectural
perspectives. The following series of photographs and drawings
illustrates this technique, which is mostly a matter of tracing.

Estimating Water Use & Water Bills

When developing a truly water-efficient design, it is very useful to
calculate the total amount of water that each zone in the design is
likely to need in a typical season. The accompanying worksheet
offers a convenient way to do this.

Estimating water bills, however, is somewhat more difficult,
because cities use many different methods for calculating water
bills, and because water rates change frequently. One current
trend is to charge higher rates for greater use of water in order to
encourage water conservation. Many communities, however, still
charge lower rates for greater water use. A word to the wise is in
order if local water rates seem too low to worry about. Rates
almost everywhere are going up, and extraordinary increases are
not uncommon. The 1990 water rates in Lafayette, Colorado, can
be used as an example. Within the city limits of Lafayette, two
5/8-inch garden hoses running at full force (with water pressure
of 60 psi), will use water at about $3.44 per hour after monthly
water use has reached the highest water rate. Outside the city
limits, this would double to about $6.88 per hour. These are
among the highest rates in the Rocky Mountain region. In
Boulder, Colorado, which has some of the lowest rates, the same
two hoses would use water at a rate of about $1.20 per hour. The
city of Lafayette reports that some customers had water bills of
more than $1000 in June 1990.

The following three designs, created for the same property,
illustrate how significantly water use, and resulting water bills, are
affected by different designs. These designs are based on the site
inventory and analysis and diagrammatic design illustrated in the
previous section of this chapter.

Computation of water use and water bills for Lafayette are
included to illustrate the use of the worksheet. Rates for several
other areas are included to give an idea of the range of water costs
around the Rocky Mountain region between 1988 and 1990.
Construction costs in this study were based on estimates of two
landscape contractors who were asked to review the designs and
prepare bids.

This sequence of photos
and drawings illustrates an
almost foolproof way to try out
design ideas.

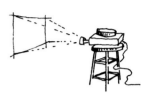

Step One: Start by projecting a
slide of the area to be designed
onto a piece of paper. In this case
the idea is to create an arbor that
will partially block the view from
the neighbor's kitchen windows.

Step Two: Trace the major
existing elements in the scene.

Step Three: Locate the vanishing point (the spot lines converge toward), then construct any architectural elements that are needed. It is often best to work on tracing paper overlays at this stage to avoid cluttering up the original line drawing while the architectural elements are worked out.

Step Four: Develop the new design by adding or subtracting such elements as shrubs and trees. It is also easy to change seasons by adding or erasing leaves on deciduous plants. Again, it is often best to work on tracing paper overlays until the desired design is worked out.

The results show that the final design looks like the sketches, because the sketches were based on the actual landscape.

SINGLE FAMILY RESIDENTIAL RATES

Lafayette, Colorado, 1990 water rates	Inside City	Outside City
First 5,000 gallons	$13.25	$26.50
Second 5,000 gallons	$ 1.75/1,000 gal.	$ 3.50/1,000 gal.
Third 5,000 gallons	$ 2.27/1,000 gal.	$ 4.54/1,000 gal.
Fourth 5,000 gallons	$ 3.02/1,000 gal.	$ 6.04/1,000 gal.
Over 20,000 gallons	$ 4.10/1,000 gal.	$ 8.20/1,000 gal.

Boulder, Colorado, 1990	Inside City	Outside City
Block 1 (for amts. less than 100% of avg. winter use)	$ .81/1,000 gal.	$ .89/1,000 gal.
Block 2 (for amts. greater than 100% but less than 400% of avg. winter use)	$ .99/1,000 gal.	$ 1.09/1,000 gal.
Block 3 (for amts. greater than 400% of avg. winter use)	$ 1.43/1,000 gal.	$ 1.57/1,000 gal.

Santa Fe, New Mexico, 1988 (throughout water distict)	
First 5,000 gallons	$ 2.97/1,000 gal.
More than 5,000 gallons	$ 3.47/1,000 gal.

Flagstaff, Arizona, 1990	Inside City	Outside City
First 12,000 gallons	$ 2.65/1,000 gal.	$ 5.30/1,000 gal.
More than 12,000 gallons	$ 3.50/1,000 gal.	$ 8.00/1,000 gal.

Notes on water bill calculations:

1. Cities often add one or more fixed charges (for such things as meter reading) to the water cost each month, which must be paid regardless of how little water is used.

2. Sewer and stormwater utility charges are often combined with water bills.

3. The computations on the following worksheets are based on outdoor water use over a period of five months, and are based on rates for Lafayette, Colorado, outside the city limits.

WORKSHEET FOR ESTIMATING LANDSCAPE WATER USE

1. **HIGH WATERING ZONES:** (18 to 20 gallons/square foot/
   20-week season)
   Lawn (Kentucky Bluegrass) . . . . _____ square feet
   Shrubs . . . . _____ square feet
   Groundcovers . . . . _____ square feet
   Flowers. . . . . _____ square feet
   Other. . . . . _____ square feet

   Total for High Watering Zones. . . . . . _____ square feet
   <u>x 18 gallons/square foot</u>

   Total 20-week usage for
   High Watering Zones . . . . _____ gallons

2. **MODERATE WATERING ZONES:** (10 ± gallons/square
   foot/20-week season)
   Lawn (Turf-type Tall Fescue or
   Crested Wheatgrass) . . . . _____ square feet
   Shrubs . . . . _____ square feet
   Groundcovers . . . . _____ square feet
   Flowers. . . . . _____ square feet
   Other. . . . . _____ square feet

   Total for Moderate Watering Zones . . _____ square feet
   <u>x 10 gallons/square foot</u>

   Total 20-week usage for
   Moderate Watering Zones . . . . _____ gallons

3. **LOW WATERING ZONES:** (0 to 3 gallons/square foot/
   20-week season)
   Lawn (Buffalograss or
   Blue Grama) . . . . _____ square feet
   Shrubs . . . . _____ square feet
   Groundcovers . . . . _____ square feet
   Flowers. . . . . _____ square feet
   Other. . . . . _____ square feet

   Total for Low Watering Zones . . . . . . _____ square feet
   <u>x 3 gallons/square foot</u>

   Total 20-week usage for
   Low Watering Zones. . . . . _____ gallons

**TOTAL 20-WEEK LANDSCAPE
WATER USAGE** (1 + 2 + 3) . . . . _____ gallons

Sample Water Use & Water Bill Computations

EXAMPLE #1:

Xeriscape, Foothills-style Design

This Xeriscape design would look much like the natural landscape along the foothills on the west side of Boulder, Colorado, or the east side of Taos, New Mexico, as well as some areas near Salt Lake City, Utah, and Flagstaff, Arizona. Maintenance would be very easy; the small, watered lawn would require only about five minutes to mow, and the rest of the yard would not require regular, weekly maintenance. Because the only areas that require regular watering are so small, the need for an expensive automatic sprinkler system is eliminated. Adequate water can be supplied by two settings of a manual hose-end sprinkler, plus a simple do-it-yourself system that hooks to the end of a hose and is left in place in the garden.

Construction of this design would be relatively inexpensive, because much of the site is seeded, rather than sodded, and many of the shrubs and flowers could be of small sizes.

Original installation cost:	$ .93/square foot
Water use (20-week season):	2568 gallons
Water cost (20-week season):	$133.00 (min. possible charge)

Foothills Style Xeriscape Design: Plants visible in this late August photo of a xeric zone flower area include Russian Sage (*Perovskia atriplicifolia*), Blackfoot Daisy (*Melampodium leucanthum*), Dakota Verbena (*Verbena bipinnatifida*), California Poppies (*Eschscholzia californica*). Shrubs include Blue and Green Rabbitbrush (*Chrysothamnus spp.*), Bluemist Spirea (*Caryopteris* × *clandonensis*).

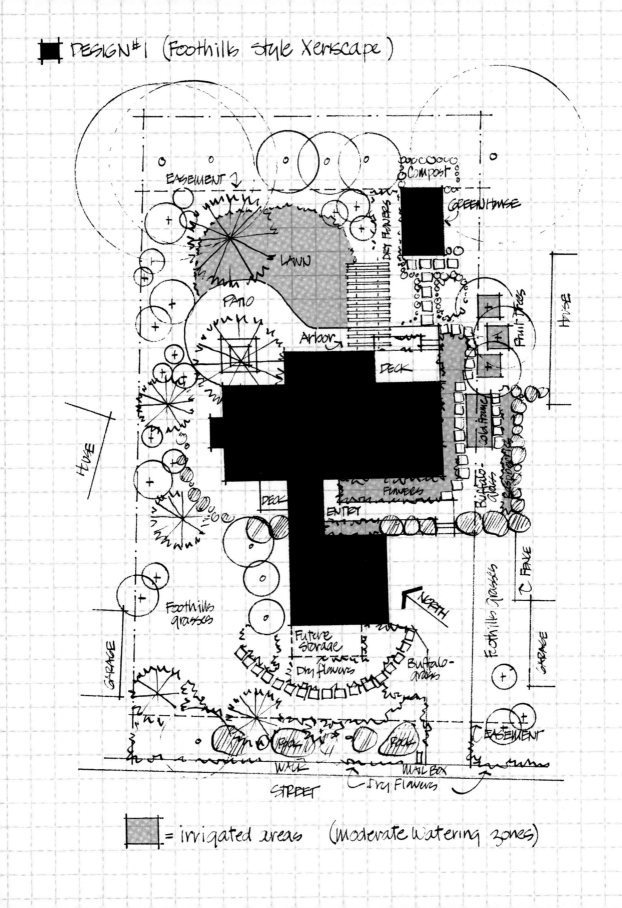

■ DESIGN#1 (Foothills Style Xeriscape)

EASEMENT

Compost

GREENHOUSE

LAWN

DRY FLOWERS

PATIO

Arbor →

DECK

Fruit Trees

HOUSE

DECK

Flowers

Joie France

Buffalo Grass

Buffalo Grass

Respberries

ENTRY

HIVE

NORTH

Foothills Grasses

FENCE

GARAGE

Foothills Grasses

Future Storage

Dry Flowers

Buffalo Grass

GARAGE

HIVE

GARAGE

EASEMENT

ROCK   ROCK

WALL

MAIL BOX

STREET

Dry Flowers

■ = irrigated areas   (moderate watering zones)

Part One: Estimating Water Use

1. **HIGH WATERING ZONES:** (18 to 20 gallons/square foot/ 20-week season)

   Lawn (Kentucky Bluegrass) . . . . _____ square feet

   Shrubs . . . . _____ square feet

   Groundcovers . . . . _____ square feet

   Flowers. . . . . _____ square feet

   Other. . . . . _____ square feet

   Total for High Watering Zones. . . . . . _____ square feet
   x 18 gallons/square foot

   Total 20-week usage for
   High Watering Zones . . . . _____ gallons

2. **MODERATE WATERING ZONES:** (10 ± gallons/square foot/20-week season)

   Lawn (Turf-type Tall Fescue or
   Crested Wheatgrass). . . . . *1048* square feet

   Shrubs . . . . *—* square feet

   Groundcovers . . . . *—* square feet

   Flowers. . . . . *512* square feet

   Other. . . . . *—* square feet

   Total for Moderate Watering Zones . . *1560* square feet
   x 10 gallons/square foot

   Total 20-week usage for
   Moderate Watering Zones . . . . *15,600* gallons

3. **LOW WATERING ZONES:** (0 to 3 gallons/square foot/ 20-week season)

   Lawn (Buffalograss or
   Blue Grama) . . . . *128* square feet

   Shrubs . . . . *—* square feet

   Groundcovers . . . . *—* square feet

   Flowers. . . . . *728* square feet

   Other. . . . . *—* square feet

   Total for Low Watering Zones . . . . . . *856* square feet
   x 3 gallons/square foot

   Total 20-week usage for
   Low Watering Zones. . . . . *2568* gallons

   **TOTAL 20-WEEK LANDSCAPE
   WATER USAGE** (1 + 2 + 3) . . . . *18,168* gallons

**Part Two:
Estimating
the Water Bill**

18,168 total gallons for one season

5 months (typical watering season) at $26.50 (for first 5,000 gallons each month) = $132.50

$26.50 = minimum monthly charge regardless of how little water is used.

FUTURE LANDSCAPE WATER CONSERVATION ORDINANCES ARE LIKELY TO BE VERY STRICT

A landscape water conservation ordinance being considered by Reno, Nevada, illustrates what is likely to lie ahead for many more communities. Turf restrictions in this proposed ordinance would include:

1. No turf in parking area landscaping.
2. No turf composed of less than 60% Turf-type Tall Fescue. In other words, no pure Kentucky Bluegrass.
3. No turf on mounds.
4. No turf in landscape areas less than 10 feet wide.

Sample maximum turf allowances would include:

1. Commercial   5%
2. Industrial   5%
3. Multi-family   15%
4. Residential   10%

It is not clear in the draft version of the ordinance whether Blue Grama and Buffalograss would be included in these restrictions, or whether these would be considered meadow landscaping and therefore exemptions. ∎

EXAMPLE #2:

Xeriscape, Suburban-style Design

This Xeriscape design would look like typical, "manicured and clipped" suburban subdivision landscaping. It illustrates that the Xeriscape approach to design provides the possibility of creating almost any appearance that might be desired. Maintenance would be somewhat more than for the foothills design in Example #1, but would be considerably less than for the Kentucky Bluegrass design in Example #3, because the Buffalograss lawn and other areas require far less regular maintenance than Kentucky Bluegrass.

Original Installation Cost: $1.09/square foot
Water Use (20-week season):   19,316 gallons
Water Cost (20-week season): $133.00 (min. possible charge)

Suburban Style Xeriscape Design: Flowers in this October photo include: Paper Flower (*Psilostrophe tagetina*), Double Bubble Mint (*Agastache cana*), 'Burgundy' Gaillardia (*Gaillardia* × *'Burgundy'*), Santa Fe Aster (*Machaeranthera bigelovii*), and Snow-in-summer (*Cerastium tomentosum*).

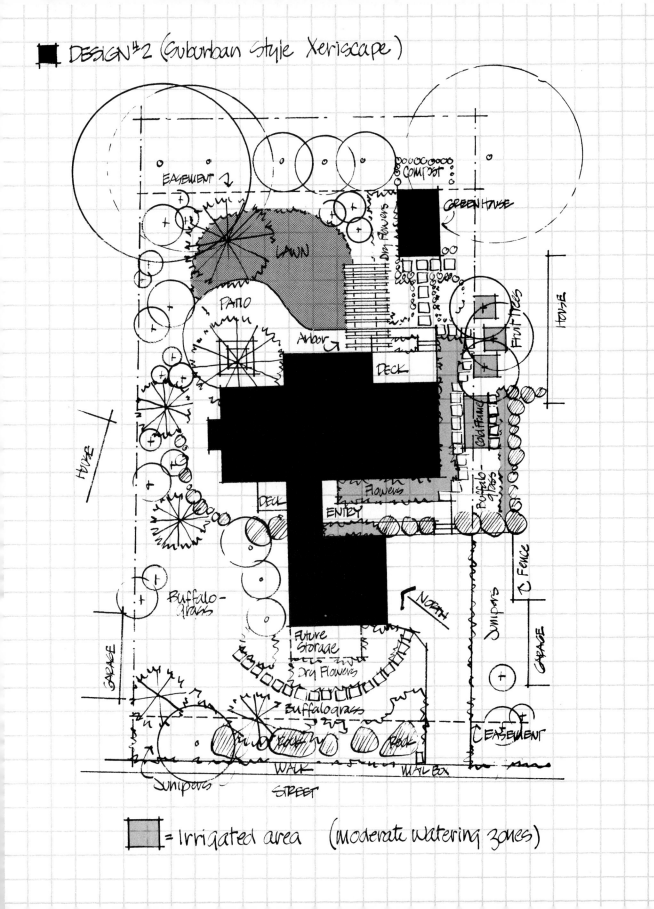

■ DESIGN #2 (Suburban Style Xeriscape)

EASEMENT

COMPOST

GREENHOUSE

LAWN

Dry Flowers

HOUSE

PATIO

Arbor

Fruit Trees

DECK

HOUSE

Cold Frame

Flowers

Buffalo-grass

DECK

ENTRY

Fence

Future Storage
Dry Flowers

NORTH

Buffalo-grass

Junipers

Buffalograss

GARAGE

GARAGE

EASEMENT

Junipers

WALK

MAIL Box

STREET

☐ = Irrigated area   (Moderate watering zones)

**Part One:
Estimating
Water Use**

1. **HIGH WATERING ZONES:** (18 to 20 gallons/square foot/
20-week season)
Lawn (Kentucky Bluegrass) . . . . _____ square feet
Shrubs . . . . _____ square feet
Groundcovers . . . . _____ square feet
Flowers. . . . . _____ square feet
Other. . . . . _____ square feet

Total for High Watering Zones. . . . . . _____ square feet
x 18 gallons/square foot
Total 20-week usage for
High Watering Zones . . . . _____ gallons

2. **MODERATE WATERING ZONES:** (10 ± gallons/square
foot/20-week season)
Lawn (Turf-type Tall Fescue or
Crested Wheatgrass) . . . . _900_ square feet
Shrubs . . . . _—_ square feet
Groundcovers . . . . _—_ square feet
Flowers. . . . . _512_ square feet
Other. . . . . _—_ square feet

Total for Moderate Watering Zones . . _1412_ square feet
x 10 gallons/square foot
Total 20-week usage for
Moderate Watering Zones . . . . _14,120_ gallons

3. **LOW WATERING ZONES:** (0 to 3 gallons/square foot/
20-week season)
Lawn (Buffalograss or
Blue Grama) . . . . _1480_ square feet
Shrubs . . . . _—_ square feet
Groundcovers . . . . _—_ square feet
Flowers. . . . . _252_ square feet
Other. . . . . _—_ square feet
Total for Low Watering Zones . . . . . . _1732_ square feet
x 3 gallons/square foot
Total 20-week usage for
Low Watering Zones. . . . . _5196_ gallons

**TOTAL 20-WEEK LANDSCAPE
WATER USAGE** (1 + 2 + 3) . . . . _19,316_ gallons

**Part Two:
Estimating
the Water Bill**

19,316 total gallons for one season

5 months (typical watering season) at $26.50 (for first 5,000 gallons each month) = $132.50

$26.50 = minimum monthly charge regardless of how little water is used.

MODERN MEDICINE FROM NATIVE PLANTS

Green Ephedra (*Ephedra viridis*), also known as Mormon Tea, is widely considered to relieve nasal congestion. Ephedrine, from this and other species, is the beneficial ingredient and has been obtained from several Asiatic species for thousands of years. *Ephedra equisetina* is one of these species. It is quite ornamental and is in cultivation in this country. The trade name Sudafed (pseudoephedrine) refers to synthetic ephedrine.

Mahonias (*Mahonia spp.*), also known as Hollygrapes, are among the most medicinally beneficial plants of the Rocky Mountain West. Most of the medicinal effects result from the yellow-colored alkaloid berberine. This chemical is associated with the intense bitter-tasting yellow color of the roots and is apparently present in direct relation to the color of the roots. It is considered very useful in reducing fevers and inflammatory conditions. It is also used as a laxative, an antibacterial skin wash, and a liver stimulant. There are reports that it is an excellent hangover remedy. The flowers are considered useful as an effective skin dressing for reducing skin infections. Berberine, in combination with quinine, has been reported to be the first modern treatment for malaria. The berberine not only helps suppress the dangerous malarial fevers, but also releases the malaria parasites from tissues, so that complete treatment of the underlying parasitic infection can be accomplished. ■

EXAMPLE #3:

Typical Kentucky Bluegrass-Dominated Design

This design would look like most suburban landscaping from coast to coast, because it is dominated by watered, manicured lawn. The large lawn would require several hours of mowing and trimming at least once per week for up to five months. Missing a mowing, for even a few days, would be immediately apparent. The design would require an expensive and extensive automatic irrigation system because of the complexity and extent of the areas requiring watering up to three times per week.

Original Installation Cost:	$1.14/square foot
Water Use (20-week season):	137,016 gallons
Water Cost (20-week season):	$998.00

"Lawnscape" Style Design: A quintessential example of the landscape style so familiar throughout the Rocky Mountain region. Plants include Kentucky Bluegrass and various junipers.

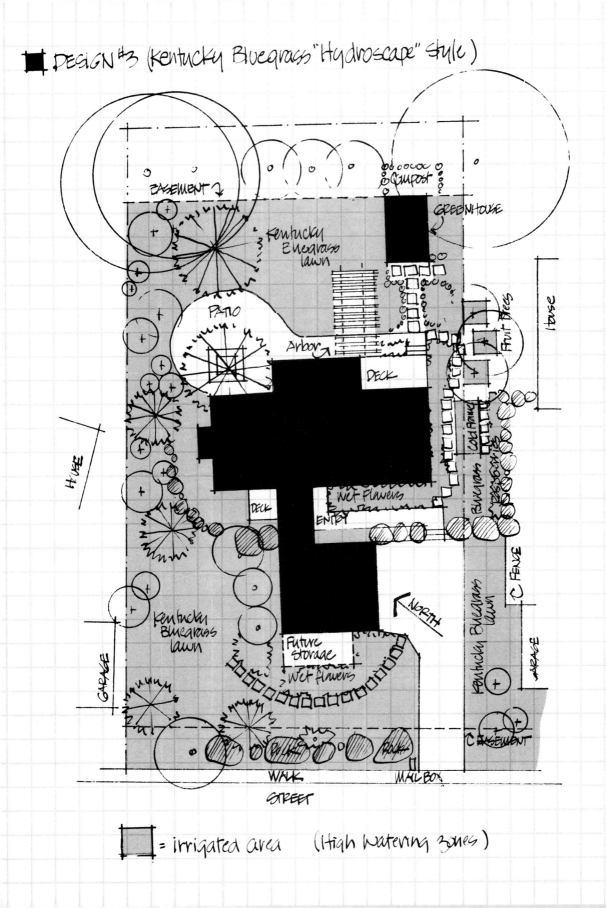

■ DESIGN #3 (Kentucky Bluegrass "Hydroscape" Style)

EASEMENT

COMPOST

GREENHOUSE

Kentucky Bluegrass lawn

House

PATIO

Fruit Trees

Arbor

DECK

HOUSE

Cold Frame

Bluegrass

WET Flowers

DECK

ENTRY

NORTH

Kentucky Bluegrass lawn

C FENCE

Future Storage

Kentucky Bluegrass lawn

WET Flowers

GARAGE

GARAGE

C EASEMENT

WALK

MAIL BOX

STREET

☐ = irrigated area   (High Watering Zones)

**Part One:
Estimating
Water Use**

1. **HIGH WATERING ZONES:** (18 to 20 gallons/square foot/
20-week season)

Lawn (Kentucky Bluegrass) . . . . __*5704*__ square feet

Shrubs . . . . __*1120*__ square feet

Groundcovers . . . . __*276*__ square feet

Flowers . . . . __*512*__ square feet

Other . . . . __*—*__ square feet

Total for High Watering Zones . . . . . . __*7612*__ square feet

x 18 gallons/square foot

Total 20-week usage for
High Watering Zones . . . . __*137,016*__ gallons

2. **MODERATE WATERING ZONES:** (10 ± gallons/square
foot/20-week season)

Lawn (Turf-type Tall Fescue or
Crested Wheatgrass) . . . . _____ square feet

Shrubs . . . . _____ square feet

Groundcovers . . . . _____ square feet

Flowers . . . . _____ square feet

Other . . . . _____ square feet

Total for Moderate Watering Zones . . _____ square feet

x 10 gallons/square foot

Total 20-week usage for
Moderate Watering Zones . . . . _____ gallons

3. **LOW WATERING ZONES:** (0 to 3 gallons/square foot/
20-week season)

Lawn (Buffalograss or
Blue Grama) . . . . _____ square feet

Shrubs . . . . _____ square feet

Groundcovers . . . . _____ square feet

Flowers . . . . _____ square feet

Other . . . . _____ square feet

Total for Low Watering Zones . . . . . . _____ square feet

x 3 gallons/square foot

Total 20-week usage for
Low Watering Zones . . . . _____ gallons

**TOTAL 20-WEEK LANDSCAPE
WATER USAGE** (1 + 2 + 3) . . . . . . __*137,016*__ gallons

Part Two:
Estimating
the Water Bill

137,016	total gallons for one season	
– 25,000	(5 months at $26.50/first	
	5000 gallons each month)	$132.50
112,016	gallons	
– 5,000	(5,000 gallons at $3.50/1000 gallons)	$ 17.50
107,016	gallons	
– 5,000	(5,000 gallons at $4.54/1000 gallons)	$ 22.70
102,016	gallons	
– 5,000	(5,000 gallons at $6.04/1000 gallons)	$ 30.20
97,016	(97,016 gallons at $8.20/1000 gallons)	$795.00
	Total	$998.00

Notes:

Five months is a good average for outdoor watering in the Denver Metro area.

Because of extreme fluctuations (due to extreme weather variations), water usage from month to month can vary greatly. Because of this, only the first 5,000 gallons each month could realistically be estimated. The remaining total water use was treated as a single month when considering the block rate. Computing this as five separate months might result in a slightly smaller total.

MONARCH MIGRATIONS

Next time there is a monarch butterfly in your yard, consider the annual trek of these tiny but mighty creatures.

With the end of each summer season, survival of the monarch species is dependent on the successful, but still poorly understood, ability of these tiny creatures to migrate to winter sites in coastal California, central Mexico, or possibly Florida.

To make such long journeys (which may cover 1,800 miles or more) even more amazing, the monarchs that return south are not the same individuals that flew north in the spring! However, approximately 1 percent of the overwintering generation survives to begin the northward journey in the spring.

The monarch winter refuge in Mexico, discovered in 1974, consists of only thirteen sites scattered about in a seventy-five- by thirty-five-mile area west of Mexico City. With only a few additional winter sites in California, and possibly a few in Florida, this butterfly species is very vulnerable to human habitat destruction. Considerable favorable public attention is needed to stimulate protection efforts that would enable the monarchs to survive, and to continue to amaze the world with their remarkable migration abilities. ■

3.

BUILDING WATERWISE GARDENS

*E*ach garden presents different questions
about what to do first, how much to do
all at once, what to do over an extended
period of time, and even in what sequence
to do things. Initial weed control and soil
preparation, however, are "now or never"
things that always need to be considered at
the start. How much to do all at once is
largely an individual decision, but it may
be helpful to point out that a large garden,
prepared all at one time, need not be
planted all at once. A few plants, grouped
attractively, can provide a good start for a
large garden that will be planted over an
extended period. This chapter covers the
various aspects of building a waterwise
garden, presented more or less in the order
in which they are usually encountered. ■

Removing Existing Grass

 If the area being prepared has been a lawn, it is best to strip off the old grass manually or with a mechanical sod stripper. The sod that is removed can be composted for later use, although composting sod takes a long time. It could also be used to build earth mounds, or it might even be used for a new lawn elsewhere. Tilling existing lawn grass into the future flower bed will almost certainly result in a long-term weed problem when it reestablishes itself among the flowers. Killing the original turf with an herbicide will still leave the difficult problem of tilling the thick dead turf into an acceptable texture, and there is increasing evidence that popular herbicides (such as "Round Up," which is based on the widely recommended chemical glyphosate) can cause troublesome problems. It is reported that the glyphosate can become "tied-up" in the dead vegetation, causing problems later, when the dead vegetation is tilled into the soil.

If the area has been a meadow of long grasses, it usually must be dug by hand, because the roots are likely to be so deep that rototilling by itself will probably not eliminate them. The old meadow grasses and roots, however, make good compost.

Soil Preparation: Don't Overdo It

Ultimately, gardening success depends on proper attention to the type of soil in which the plants are growing. There is an old saying, "Be sure the roots have what they need, and the tops will take care of themselves." This may involve elaborate soil amendments in order to adjust the situation to meet the needs of the plants, or by adjusting the plant selection to the soil conditions, it may require no soil preparation at all. Growing rhododendrons in the Rocky Mountain states, for example, usually requires very elaborate soil preparation. Growing Buffalograss in "Denver adobe" (heavy clay), however, does not; Buffalograss actually likes heavy clay.

As with most things in life, the best approach to soil preparation is usually somewhere between doing nothing and attempting to do too much. Generally, most of the attention should be paid to soil structure, rather than to fertility. If there is need to work with fertility, it can usually be done later, but soil structure is very difficult to alter in an established garden. The structure of most soil in the Rocky Mountain states is either too sandy or has too much clay. The answer in either case is to add organic matter such as compost or *well-aged* manure. The type of manure (chicken, cow, sheep, and so on) is less important than its age. "Fresh," or new, manure can contain too much nitrogen and salt. Because many arid and semiarid plants are especially sensitive to the high nitrogen level of new manure, it is important to emphasize avoiding fresh manure. However, if fresh manure is stored outside over the winter and plowed several times, it is almost always "mellow" enough to use without problems by spring. Adding compost or manure addresses two basic requirements: the need for clay soils to absorb water more quickly while not retaining too much water and the need for sandy soils to retain more water, longer.

For most Rocky Mountain area gardeners, the following simple soil preparation steps should be adequate:

1. Use a mix of ½ good garden soil ("topsoil") and ½ compost or well-aged manure. Beware of commercially available "topsoil." Examine it before ordering any. It may be worse than what it's intended to improve. Likewise, examine manure. It may be too fresh. A half-and-half mix will usually dilute any serious problems, but check before buying and follow the principle of "buyer beware."

2. Apply the mix 2 to 3 inches deep over the area being prepared.

3. Mix the new and old soil thoroughly. Layering soil (applying soil amendments without tilling them into underlying soil) is almost always worse than doing nothing. Roots and water will not move well between layers.

Mountain Peat Problems

Strip mining of critical wetlands to obtain mountain peat should be cause for considerable concern in the Rocky Mountain states. On a single Colorado mountain peat mining site, for example, several rare plants, including *Scorpidium scorpiodes*, *Salix myrtillifolia*, *Eriophorum gracile*, *Packera* (syn. *Senecio*) *pauciflora*, *Primula egaliksensis*, and *Ptilagrostis porteri*, have recently been found. At least one of these plants (*Eriophorum gracile*) was previously thought to be extinct in Colorado, and another (*Salix myrtillifolia*) has not previously been found in the continental United States. According to David Cooper, an environmental professor at the Colorado School of Mines, these plants exist in very small and vulnerable populations, which depend on very specific habitat conditions. He points out that peat accumulates in Colorado wetlands very slowly, typically at the rate of only about eight inches per thousand years. Even more importantly, however, he considers it highly unlikely that these ecosystems could ever be deliberately restored elsewhere. There are just too many complex factors that support these ecosystems.

In addition to rare plants, these wetlands support one of the most important bird nesting habitats in the mountain West. Possibly more species nest in these areas than in any other single type of ecosystem in this region. Several mammal species, including black bear, feed extensively in these areas, and these marshlands also serve the very important function of regulating both water quality and the quantity of flow in many mountain streams.

The magnitude of the mining problem is also worth noting. Colorado is reported to rank as the fifth largest peat producer in the United States, and this includes all types of peat. Colorado, which produces only mountain peat, is the largest supplier of this product in the western United States.

Most of this peat is used as an organic soil amendment by greenhouse operations and in landscaping. Ironically, using mountain peat as a soil amendment can actually lead to problems. Among other things, the peat quality varies considerably, and there are reports of extremely high pH problems, as well as high clay content.

Fortunately, there are excellent alternatives. Various composted manure and municipal sewage products, for instance, offer much better soil amendments. Local companies, as well as an increasing number of city agencies, are turning the perennial problem of feedlot manure and city sewage sludge into profitable products worthy of support by conscientious gardeners.

It should be noted that sphagnum peat is quite different from mountain peat. Sphagnum peat is decomposed Sphagnum Moss (*Sphagnum spp.*). It is generally quite acidic and much more porous than mountain peat. Most of it comes from Canada, and although there is some controversy about mining sphagnum peat areas, it is generally much less critical than mining of mountain peat. Mountain peat is composed primarily of decomposed sedge roots. It is much less porous than sphagnum peat and tends to be basic rather than acidic.

Most of the baled "peat moss" sold in garden centers is sphagnum peat, but it is important to read the labels carefully to determine for sure what kind of peat is used. ■

Weed Control Before Planting

There is no better time for long-term weed control than before planting a new flower garden. In fact, it can literally be impossible to extricate grass from within some perennials.

One of the best methods for reducing serious annual or perennial weed problems is to till, then water and wait for the inevitable rush of weeds. This crop can then be pulled or dug, depending on the size and type of weeds involved. Tilling at this stage may actually increase problems with stoloniferous (spreading) grasses, but may be helpful with annual weeds. Herbicides can be used at this stage, but as mentioned earlier, there are reports that even glyphosate-based herbicides can cause problems. Repeating the "water-wait-weed" sequence several times may be a good idea, but the first round usually accomplishes most of what is needed.

When To Plant & Transplant

With *container grown plants*, any time you can get to it is good for planting. Don't underestimate the watering needs of plants in very hot weather, however. Plants that have been grown in potting mixes of sand and sawdust, for example, will dry out remarkably quickly in hot, dry weather. This type of soil will not draw water effectively from surrounding soil, so be prepared to water the original soil and plant directly, possibly several times daily, in severe conditions.

Deciduous shrubs and trees generally do better if dug and replanted before they leaf out in the spring. *Evergreens* also survive best if transplanted before active growth begins in the spring.

For *herbaceous perennials*, there is a lot of conflicting information about the ideal time for digging and transplanting. If the plants involved are only marginally winter hardy, it is usually best to move them one or two months before really cold weather. With other perennials, the best guide may be to wait until they have bloomed, so that the current year's bloom can be enjoyed.

All plants will do better if transplanted in cool, overcast weather. In periods of hot, sunny weather, it's best to do the work in the evening. Clay flower pots work well to shade smaller plants. They rarely, if ever, overheat. Plastic pots, however, might be a disaster in hot, sunny weather.

Finding Plants

Hunting for unusual waterwise plants can be fun or frustrating. It's rather like shopping for clothing or furniture—don't expect to find everything in one place, and try to enjoy the search.

Many of the best flowers for low watering zones have often been considered common "weeds." Plant hunting for these may require some persistence. Take Double Bubble Mint *(Agastache cana)*, for example. It smells just like old-fashioned Double Bubble bubblegum. The plant is very showy for a long time. It is easy to grow. It doesn't need much water. Hummingbirds love it. It's easy to propagate from seed, and it is considered rare and endangered in New Mexico. But, only a few New Mexico nurseries seem to know anything about it. There are a lot of other "weeds-with-potential" in this region. Chocolate Flower *(Berlandiera lyrata)* is another. Especially in the morning, it smells just like warm milk chocolate, and it blooms for a long time.

There are actually potential profits in converting these "weeds-with-potential" into coveted "designer weeds," then marketing them to Xeriscape enthusiasts. Until more of these plants are more regularly available, however, interested gardeners will have to persevere a little to find many of the best flowers for waterwise flower gardening.

There are actually many sources of unusual waterwise plants, and the list is expanding rapidly. However, some serious systematic sleuthing may be in order, since many of the best sources of unusual plants are not widely known, and new ones continually become available. The following list includes types of sources. A

CAYENNE PEPPER CONTROLS SLUGS

In a simple garden experiment, ordinary cayenne pepper (in the flaky form found commonly in shakers on tables at pizza parlors) completely eliminated slug damage. The cayenne pepper was simply sprinkled around and on the plants the slugs had been eating. Even considerable watering did not diminish the effectiveness for many weeks. ∎

more detailed list of specific agencies and companies is included in the appendix. Libraries, especially those at botanic gardens, are also good places to ask about mail-order seed and live plant sources.

Commercial nurseries. Especially when looking for unusual plants, take along photos of plants you like, and ask what they are if you are uncertain about the name. Most commercial nurseries and garden centers have at least a few people who are enthusiastic and knowledgeable about introduced and native waterwise plants. So, if the first person you encounter looks blankly at your photo of Double Bubble Mint and finally says, "a pansy will do just as well," politely excuse yourself and try again with someone else.

Some of the best commercial sources of unusual plants are wholesale rather than retail. However, items in their catalogs are usually available to the public, and it is often possible to order plants from them by "piggy backing," or combining orders with a local garden center.

Mail order. An increasing number of companies offer seeds and/or live plants by mail. See the listings in the Appendix.

Botanic garden and native plant society sales. Increasingly, this is becoming a good source of revenue for these organizations around the country. The Denver Botanic Gardens' annual plant sale each May is already a major event for Colorado plant sleuths.

Digging from the wild. Because of the extensive root systems of many arid and semiarid plants, digging wild plants is usually unsuccessful, and it is specifically illegal in many places. Digging from the wild has been compared with shoplifting—it doesn't work well, and you may get caught.

Growing Your Own Plants

Propagating your own plants (from seed, by division of established plants, or by cuttings) can be a lot of fun, and it is sometimes the only way to get unusual plants.

A short summary of propagating plants from seed at home is included here for convenience. The inevitable detailed questions that arise, when actually getting involved with this, are covered well in several sources listed in the bibliography.

When propagating plants from seed at home, the primary prerequisite is a location with adequate light. Large sunny windows or sunrooms are often ideal. Artificial light can be adequate, but plants accustomed to the bright Rocky Mountain sunlight usually don't do well for very long under artificial light. For one thing, as they grow, it is difficult to get enough light to the lower portion of the plants. An ordinary two-tube fluorescent light fixture, however, can be used successfully to get plants started for early planting in the garden.

1   **Vernalization (or stratification)** refers to the process of simu-
     lating winter by giving the seeds a period of artificial cold, damp
     conditions. It is not always easy to determine which seeds actually
     require such treatment, but some of the seed company catalogs
     and botanic garden libraries can help with this.

     Vernalization can be accomplished by putting a mixture of half
     sphagnum peat moss (not mountain peat) and half perlite in a
     plastic sandwich bag. Dampen the mix with a little water, add the
     seeds, then place the bags in a refrigerator (not freezer). Vernal-
     ization should be continued for about 2 months, but check after
     about 2 weeks. If there is evidence of germination, plant the
     seeds immediately. Only a few plants need more than 2 months
     vernalization.

2   **Germination** can be done in 4″ plastic pots with a mix of 50
     percent sphagnum peat moss and 50 percent perlite. Do not use
     peat pots, as they usually don't decompose fast enough to avoid
     inhibiting the roots after they are set in the garden. With plastic
     pots, it is easier to remove small seedlings for transplanting into
     the garden. Five to 10 days is a typical time for germination, but
     some seeds take several years! A light, well-balanced fertilizer that
     contains minor elements will be needed if plants are to be grown
     very long in this mix, because it has no fertility of its own.

3   **Transplanting seedlings**. After the seedlings have grown several
     true leaves and can be handled easily, they can be transplanted
     individually into smaller plastic pots with a mix of ⅓ sphagnum
     peat moss, ⅓ perlite, and ⅓ potting soil. It is not as important to
     use a fertilizer with minor elements when using this mix. Note:
     the sphagnum peat moss called for here is not the same thing as
     mountain peat. (See related story about mountain peat.)

     Determining when to start all of this is a challenge, but begin-
     ning vernalization in early November, then starting germination
     in early January usually results in a majority of plants being ready
     for transplanting into the garden in mid-spring.

Foreign Regions Rich in Waterwise Plants
Panayoti Kelaidis

Water conservation concerns are driving a quest for new plants that are
well-adapted to our urban landscape needs, and this leads us to search
for plants in climatic regions similar to our own. In this search, many of
the plants that have performed best in the Denver Botanic Gardens'
Rock Alpine Garden come from the floristic areas described by the
eminent Soviet botanist, M.G. Popov, as the Tethyan regions.

The term "Tethyan" is a reference to lands that originally bordered

WORKING WITH SALT-AFFECTED SOILS

According to a Colorado State University Service in Action report, three major types of salt-affected soils are *saline, sodium,* and *saline-sodium* soils.

Saline soil cannot be reclaimed with chemical amendments, condition-ers, or fertilizers. Only leaching the soil with good irrigation water can remove salts from the plant root zone of saline-affected soils, and per-manent salt removal depends on adequate drainage.

Sodium soils can be improved by replacing soil sodium with a soluble source of calcium. Sodium soils also respond well to continued application of good irrigation water, good irrigation methods, and good crop practices.

Saline-sodium affected soils presumably will respond well to good irrigation practices, but application of a soluable source of calcium may help the sodium aspect of the problem. If salt-affected soils are a prob-lem, it is highly recom-mended that a local agricultural extension service be consulted. ∎

the ancient Sea of Tethys, and which, through continental drift, now lie in widely separated areas around the world. The three principle centers of Tethyan flora are as follows:

The Madrean region includes the southwestern United States and northern Mexico.

The Mediterranean region includes southern Europe, western Asia, and northern Africa.

The Irano-Turanian region extends from Iran, five thousand miles across Soviet Central Asia, into Mongolia and central China.

Plants that grow in these regions tend to be adapted to intense sunlight, extremely variable weather, and periods of extreme drought. Working with plants from these areas, a sort of Darwinian survival of the fittest is occurring at the Denver Botanic Gardens. It appears that a new horticultural palette is emerging—one that will someday provide the local landscape industry with plants that are well adapted to our climate, and thereby will help create an attractive, sustainable regional horticulture. Promising plants from the Madrean region include:

- Mountain Mahogany species (*Cercocarpus ledifolius, C. intricatus,* and *C. brevifolius*).
- Sulphurflowers (*Eriogonum umbellatum, E. ovalifolium,* and *E. niveum*).
- Penstemons (*Penstemon strictus, P. alpinus, P. pinifolius, P. digitalis,* and *P. barbatus*).
- Prairie Zinnia (*Zinnia grandiflora*).

Promising plants from the Mediterranean region include:
- *Ptilotrichum spinosum* 'Roseum,' grown for decades in Europe and seemingly indestructible at the Denver Botanic Gardens.
- *Alyssum montanum,* similar to Basket-of-Gold (*A. saxatilis*).
- *Chamaespartium sagittale* (syn. *Genista sagittalis*), which forms a rather thick evergreen mat and has beautiful yellow blossoms.
- *Nepeta concolor,* introduced from Turkey in 1977.

Proven, but still uncommon plants from the Irano-Turanian region include:
- Central Asian Tulips, such as *Tulipa linifolia, T. turkestanica,* and *T. clusiana,* which are multiplying in Buffalograss lawns.
- Central Asian Iris, such as *Iris bucharica, I. spuria halophila,* and *I. hoogiana.*
- Salvias, such as *Salvia argentea, S. sclarea,* and *S. candidissima.*
- Hedgenettles, such as *Stachys inflata, S. alopecuros,* and *S. thirkei.*

Climatic conditions similar to those of the Tethyan regions occur in the following areas of the Southern Hemisphere:

The mountains of southern Africa, including the Cape Province and the Sudano-Zambezian-Drakensberg regions.

The mountains of New Zealand (the Neozeylandic region).

The mountains of southern South America, including the Chilean and Patagonian regions.

Hardy Yellow Ice Plant (*Delosperma nubigenum*) and Hardy Pink Ice Plant (*Delosperma cooperi*) are notable introductions from the Drakensberg Mountains.

As population in the West continues to burgeon, city planners are beginning to question the use of vast quantities of precious treated water to maintain a landscape of unadapted exotics. Native plants and those from similar climates not only need less water, but they also generally grow and survive the vicissitudes of a semiarid steppe climate much better than do plants from wetter regions.

By carefully seeking out plants from similar climatic regions, selecting superior forms, and displaying them in a public garden, we may help forge a distinctive, appropriate tradition of Rocky Mountain horticulture. ■

Panayoti Kelaidis has been curator of Denver Botanic Gardens' Rock Alpine Garden for ten years. His interests, however, extend far beyond alpine environments to include native wildflowers and drought-tolerant plants from both the Northern and Southern Hemispheres. The plant lists in Chapter 7 contain many of the plants he has successfully worked with at the Rock Alpine Garden.

Planting & Transplanting Techniques

The following principles cover many of the questions that arise either when planting individual plants into a waterwise garden (for example, after division) or transplanting new things from other locations. The idea behind these steps is to reduce sharp differences between new and old soil, so that roots and water will be able to move between the two types of soil. Be especially careful with clay soils, in which it is easy to create a "flower pot" effect that will seriously limit future growth.

1. Dig the hole several inches wider and deeper than the root mass. Don't jam the plants into very small holes, but a lot of extra room is rarely needed either.

2. Rough up the edges of the hole.

3. Rough up compacted roots of container-grown plants.

4. Back-fill around the plants with a mix of half existing soil and half amended soil, which consists of 50 percent good garden soil and 50 percent compost or well-aged manure. It's generally best not to add fertilizer at this point, because it can "burn" the roots.

5. In general, place the plants in the garden at the same level they were previously growing. A soil saucer may help retain needed water, but in some cases it may retain too much. This needs to be determined on a case-by-case basis.

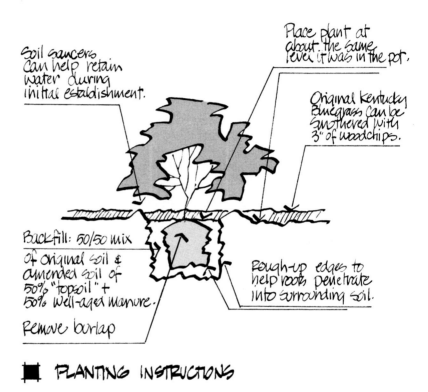

Soil saucers can help retain water during initial establishment.

Place plant at about the same level it was in the pot.

Original Kentucky Bluegrass can be smothered with 3" of woodchips.

Backfill: 50/50 mix of original soil & amended soil of 50% "topsoil" + 50% well-aged manure.

Remove burlap

Rough-up edges to help roots penetrate into surrounding soil.

■ PLANTING INSTRUCTIONS

Building Watering Systems

Automatic vs. manual, hose-end vs. underground, mini-spray vs. drip or trickle—the choices to be made in developing a truly water-efficient watering system can be somewhat bewildering. A detailed manual on irrigation design is beyond the scope of this book; the following general principles and types of systems are worth describing briefly, however.

Squares, circles, and rectangles. Consideration should be given to creating a system with sprinkler heads that will water shapes similar to the shapes in the design—square heads for square areas, circular heads for circular areas, and so on. In some cases, it may be worth refining the shapes in the design in order to fit the shapes of the available sprinkler heads better.

Low-angle, large-drop sprinkler heads. Heads that deliver water at a low angle and with large drops will reduce evaporation loss, and will reduce problems with wind blowing water out of the area of intended coverage.

Multihead coverage. This refers to the majority of the sprinkler heads available. These either water more heavily in the center of their pattern, or more heavily at the outer part of the pattern. In either case, one of the two types must be used throughout the area being watered, and 100 percent overlapping is necessary for even coverage. This type of system makes it relatively easy to water all sides of boulders in the lawn. However, there are likely to be so many heads that coverage is typically rather uneven, resulting in timing the system to apply water very heavily in order to "hide" the dry, brown spots that typically occur during heat waves.

Single-head coverage. This refers to less common systems which have heads that deliver water evenly over the pattern they are intended to cover. These systems potentially use far fewer heads, and many of the heads can be used to water from the center of a lawn area outward. Watering outward from the center can be very helpful in some situations, as illustrated in the accompanying drawing. This type of system is often especially useful for small and moderately small residential designs.

Drip-trickle-and-mini-spray. This refers to the many do-it-yourself systems (which can be found at many local garden centers) for watering groundcovers, gardens, or shrub areas. They consist of numerous parts and gadgets that allow great flexibility in design. These systems are not intended for lawn areas because the heads don't drop down to allow mowing. Most work on low pressure and can be easily adjusted for design changes or when plants grow and block the heads.

Drip irrigation. This could be described as "leaky pipe" irrigation, because it simply refers to dripping water either below ground or on the ground surface. These systems can operate either continuously or intermittently. Below ground systems are difficult to monitor for proper operation, because they are out of sight, and because it is very difficult to know how much water is being applied. Another problem is poor distribution of water at the surface, with possible oversaturation below the surface. Drip irrigation, therefore, is not appropriate for lawns, but it is useful for spot irrigation of shrubs and trees.

Hose-end systems. All of the equipment previously mentioned can be used with conventional hoses, and the following accessories will make a well-considered hose-end system a very easy and inexpensive way to water efficiently.

Quick couple devices attached to hose ends and sprinklers make

UNEVEN- VS. EVEN-COVERAGE SPRINKLERS

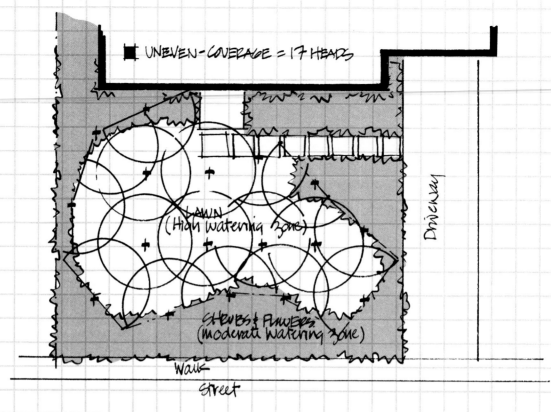

UNEVEN-COVERAGE = 17 HEADS

LAWN
(High watering zone)

SHRUBS & FLOWERS
(Moderate watering zone)

Walk

Street

Driveway

Typical uneven-coverage sprinklers require 100% overlap to accomplish even watering.

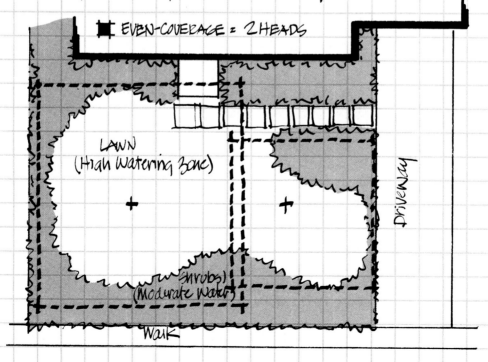

EVEN-COVERAGE = 2 HEADS

LAWN
(High Watering Zone)

Shrubs)
(Moderate Water)

Walk

Driveway

changing hoses and accessories very convenient. *Faucet shut-off devices* are inexpensive and will reliably shut off water after the gardener has gone to work or to bed. *Automatic faucet shut-off and turn-on devices* are relatively more expensive devices that reliably turn hoses on and off several times daily, or weekly, and are powered by flashlight batteries.

Underground automatic systems. Thorough coverage of the intricacies of the timers, valves, and pipes used in this rapidly changing, high-tech aspect of irrigation is beyond the scope of this book but is well covered in many other sources. In general, it can be estimated that several hundred dollars will obtain the best hose-end equipment that money will buy, while it will require several thousand dollars to buy an adequate underground automatic system.

Using Watering Systems Efficiently

Having a good system (whether manual or automatic) is important, but understanding how to use it well is just as important. The following items cover most of the important considerations in using a watering system efficiently.

1   **Determine how much water is needed and how often each watering zone needs watering.** The waterwise watering zones described in Chapter 1 are good guides in determining how much water is needed and how often it should be applied. Each garden, however, will require some experimentation with the guidelines to compensate for unusual sun, slope, or soil factors.

Evapo-transpiration (ET) rates are published in regional newspapers and on television as a guide to how much water is needed under current conditions. They are based on analysis of solar radiation, wind, humidity, recent rainfall, and so on, and can be good indicators, but they must be understood to be useful. *First,* they are usually calculated only for Kentucky Bluegrass, not for Turf-type Tall Fescue or Buffalograss lawns. *Second,* it is important to know whether the rates are calculated for each day, or for several days (to correspond to watering schedules of every other day or every third day). *Third,* it is best to withhold watering until at least ½ inch is called for, because watering less than ½ inch is not likely to result in replacing water in the root zone, where roots have been removing water. *Fourth,* published ET rates do not take into account different soil types or slopes. Sandy, sunny slopes, for example, need more watering than shady, level clay areas. *Fifth,* adjusting automatic systems for average monthly ET rates can be very effective in increasing the overall efficiency of automatic irrigation. The accompanying chart illustrates how much the average ET rate changes through the irrigation season in Denver.

2   Determine how long to water. Once the quantity and frequency of watering is determined, it is important to know how long to run a system to deliver that amount of water. This can be done by setting several rain gauges (or straight-sided soup or tuna cans) under the sprinklers and timing how long it takes to deliver the amount of water that is needed. By doing this in several locations in a watering zone, it is possible to determine whether the general coverage is reasonably even.

3   Determine how fast to water. Ideally, this should be done before installing a system, so that heads can be selected for proper watering rates in the area they cover. However, if the system is already installed and runoff is a problem, it may be necessary to experiment with watering for several short periods to avoid runoff.

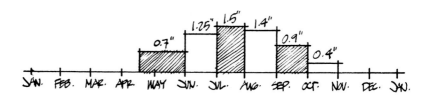

■ ADJUST AUTOMATIC ~~SYSTEMS~~ MONTHLY

this information illustrates that it is important
to adjust automatic irrigation systems at least
monthly. the information in this chart is based
on Denver area average Kentucky Bluegrass
ET rates, & indicates the amount of water to
apply each week.

INDOOR WATER USE ADDS UP TOO!

TYPICAL DAILY WATER USE PER PERSON

Toilets	40%	30 gallons
Showers	32%	25 gallons
Laundry	10%	8 gallons
Dish washing	5%	4 gallons
Cooking	5%	4 gallons
Tooth brushing	4%	3 gallons
Cleaning	4%	3 gallons
	100%	77 gallons (not counting irrigation)

Note: Some areas in California are considering limiting 1991 water use to 50 gallons per person per day (including irrigation).

TOILET FACTS

A standard toilet uses $3\frac{1}{2}$ to 7+ gallons per flush.

An average adult flushes the toilet 6 times daily.

An average household flushes 15–20 times daily.

A silent toilet leak can use 40+ gallons daily.

ULTRA LOW-FLOW TOILETS VS. RETRO-FIT DEVICES

Ultra low-flow units cost from $100 to $300, not counting installation.

Good retro-fit devices cost about $30, are do-it-yourself, use as little as $1\frac{1}{2}$ gallons per flush (same as good ultra low-flow toilets), and provide big flushes when needed—no "skid marks," no "grounded flounders," and no plugged plumbing.

SHOWER FACTS

Standard heads use 5–8 gallons/minute at full pressure.

Low-flow heads use $1\frac{1}{2}$–3 gallons/minute at full pressure.

HOT WATER FACTS

Three quarts to 4 gallons may be used before hot water reaches a faucet. Consider catching this in a pail for use in the garden.

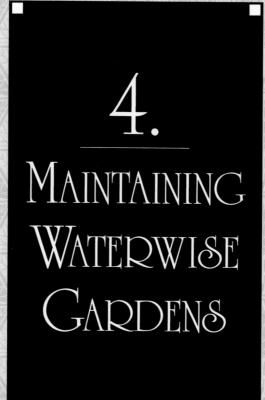

4.

MAINTAINING WATERWISE GARDENS

In a competition between traditional lawns and waterwise flower gardens (based on maintenance-time-per-square-foot), the waterwise flower garden is very likely to win by a surprisingly large margin. Just as important as savings in total maintenance time, however, flower garden maintenance can be scheduled much more flexibly than maintenance of manicured lawns. ■

Waterwise Flowers vs. Traditional Lawns

 Much of the myth that flower garden maintenance is very demanding is based on misconceptions about watering, weeding, deadheading (removing seed heads), and replacing plants. In reality, all of these tasks can be quite enjoyable, and very importantly, they can be done when it is convenient, because neglecting such tasks doesn't show immediately.

Manicured lawns, on the other hand, will immediately show neglect if not mowed, trimmed, and watered at least weekly. Well-designed, waterwise flower gardens, by comparison, can frequently be left unattended for many weeks with no ill effects.

Knowing how to make the most of the potentially reduced maintenance of arid and semiarid flower gardening is based on some understanding of how plants cope with dry conditions.

Thriving on Less: The Drought Defenses of Plants

Drought-tolerant, drought-escaping, drought-demanding, drought-avoiding, truly drought-tolerant—the number of terms referring to various drought-coping adaptations of plants is at least as great as the number of arguments about which terms are appropriate.

It is especially important to keep in mind that the term "drought-tolerant" is commonly used in many different ways. For example, it is sometimes used to refer to plants that are able to thrive in a dry region without any irrigation, or it may simply mean that a plant needs only a little irrigation. Confusion arises when, for example, a plant is called drought-tolerant in Indianapolis, without recognizing that it may need considerable irrigation in Salt Lake City. Most of the confusion, however, can be eliminated by consciously considering how a term is being used in each case.

The considerable array of terms used in referring to how plants cope with various dry conditions reflects the many evolutionary adaptations that occur in nature, and some understanding of this can serve the waterwise gardener very well.

Consider, for example, traditional Kentucky Bluegrass lawns and the increasingly popular Turf-type Tall Fescue lawns. Bluegrass is relatively shallow rooted, and Tall Fescue is relatively deep rooted. There are reports that Bluegrass root zones should be considered in inches while Turf-type Tall Fescue root zones should be considered in feet. The significance of this in water-efficient landscaping is that relatively frequent, light irrigation best serves Bluegrass lawns, while relatively less frequent, heavier irrigation best serves Turf-type Tall Fescue lawns. More specifically, in the Denver area, Kentucky Bluegrass often needs ½ inch of water three times per week, while Tall Fescue lawns need only ¾ inch

COMMERCIAL NECTAR TURNS OFF HUMMINGBIRDS

Aelred Geis, director of research for Wild Bird Centers, Inc., reports that tests he has done show that a homemade water and sugar solution is greatly preferred over two major commercial solutions. The recommended solution is 4:1 (water to sugar). Coloring is not necessary, but it may be helpful initially. More sugar is NOT recommended, since it may result in enlarging the bird's liver (which can be fatal), and because it may also lure the birds too much away from their natural food sources.

Honey should NOT be used, since birds lack the enzymes needed for digesting it, and because they can get a disease from honey, which can destroy their tongues and therefore their ability to feed. ■

of water once per week under similar conditions. Note that both the frequency and the amount of water vary considerably.

The differences in these two grasses also appear when trying to use evapo-transpiration (ET) ratings effectively. If a deep-rooted Turf-type Tall Fescue lawn is watered at correct Fescue ET rates (in ¼-inch, frequent applications), the lawn may still turn brown, because the roots draw water from well below the surface, while the irrigation water is being applied at the surface in quantities too small to reach the roots. Waiting until at least ½ inch of water is indicated is likely to yield better results. Conversely, if a shallow-rooted Bluegrass lawn (especially if growing on sandy soil) is watered once per week with the accumulated correct ET rate, much of the water is likely to drain deep into the soil, beyond the roots. Again, the result is likely to be a brown lawn.

Another example involves central Asian flowering bulbs such as tulips, irises, alliums, fritillarias, and eremurus. These showy plants have evolved under conditions of extreme summer drought (sometimes no rain for many months) and abundant winter moisture. This suggests that summer watering may even be detrimental to these plants, and extremely well-drained soil may be very important. This is partially verified by observing that some of these plants are thriving in Rocky Mountain Buffalograss lawns, where they add considerable color in the spring before the Buffalograss turns green.

Another lesson is apparent in observing that along the Colorado Front Range, where the annual precipitation is similar to many areas in central Asia, very wet weather or very dry weather can come at any time of year. This results in a greater abundance of summer wildflowers and perennial grasses than in central Asia. Many of these summer wildflowers cope with the unpredictable dry conditions by not blooming as freely, or even dying back temporarily, when it is dry. This suggests that a little irrigation, applied only in the driest times, is probably all that is needed for reliable results with these plants.

Still other plants in this area bridge the dry spells by storing considerable quantities of water in extensive root systems. Bush Morning Glory (*Ipomoea leptophylla*) is an extreme example of this. Excavated roots of this plant have been reported to weigh one hundred pounds and extend fifteen to twenty feet in various directions. Plants like this may not need irrigation anywhere in the Rocky Mountain region and may fail to thrive if given even moderate irrigation.

A familiarity with the vast array of arid conditions plants encounter and the innumerable methods that have evolved to enable them to thrive in these varied conditions will help clever

CAN PLANTS ABSORB WATER DIRECTLY THROUGH THEIR LEAVES?

Despite some controversy about direct absorption of water in various plant species, it is apparent that bromeliads (*Bromeliaceae*) do absorb liquid water directly through their leaves. One genus (*Bromeliaceae tillandsia spp.*) is so successful at this that it manages to inhabit the essentially rainless Atacama desert of northern Chile and southern Peru by condensing and absorbing fog from the Pacific Ocean directly through its leaves. Most plants, however, do not absorb water directly through their leaves, and must depend on adequate soil moisture for survival. ∎

gardeners to put the right plant in the right place. For this reason, it is worthwhile to consider the following list of specialized drought-coping adaptations:

Specialized roots. *Deep root systems* allow plants to draw from permanent ground water. Poppy Mallow (*Callirhoe involucrata*) is a good example. It may never need irrigation to perform well and frequently does poorly with even moderate levels of irrigation. Conversely, *shallow roots* are helpful in making use of frequent light summer rains. Many plants combine the advantages of both deep and shallow roots. Yuccas use this strategy and get along in most areas with no supplemental irrigation.

Some plants make use of *rapidly regenerating roots*. The new Turf-type Tall Fescue grasses are reported to be able to regenerate roots and redistribute root growth in rapid response to available soil moisture. *Tubers, rhizomes, and bulbs* are among various means of storing water for use in dry spells. Bush Morning Glory (*Ipomoea leptophylla*), with its hundred-pound roots, and many irises use this strategy very effectively.

The *root-to-top ratio* of a plant is another drought defense. Many arid land plants develop root systems much more expansive than their tops. Bur Oaks (*Quercus macrocarpa*) are reported to develop just two leaves from stored reserves in the acorn, then grow a tap root sometimes three feet in length before growing any more leaves. Grasses may develop several miles of roots to cope with frequent dry weather. The record holder for deep roots, however, is likely to be Mesquite (*Prosopis juliflora*) with depths to 175 feet being reported.

Specialized leaves. *Light color* is very common in plants from sunny, arid regions. Presumably this reflects light and helps keep the leaves cool, allowing metabolic activity to continue when it otherwise would be too hot. Buffalograss, Blue Grama, and Crested Wheatgrass are all from semiarid regions and are lighter colored than Kentucky Bluegrass, which is adapted to wetter areas. *Fuzzy or hairy leaves* are another adaptation that is almost as common as light color, and may serve to reduce wind velocity as well as to provide a little shade on the leaves. Many of the salvias have this characteristic.

Curling and rolling leaves can also help plants survive dry and hot conditions. Curl-leaf Mountain Mahogany (*Cercocarpus ledifolius*) has permanently curled leaves that reduce exposure to hot sun and wind. Many grasses roll and unroll their leaves in response to changing conditions. Other plants feature *waxy and scurfy leaf coatings*. Wild Four O'Clock (*Mirabilis multiflora*) has thick, waxy leaves, and Four-wing Saltbush (*Atriplex canescens*) has scurfy leaf surfaces to reduce evaporation.

Stomatal control is demonstrated by many cactus species, which take in carbon dioxide through their stomata during the cool evening hours and store it for use in photosynthesis during the day, when the stomata are closed to reduce evaporation.

Green stems characterize the drought adaptations of some Rocky Mountain plants. Mormon Tea (*Ephedra viridis*) is a good example of a plant that reduces surface area by photosynthesizing with its stems, rather than with leaves. *Succulent leaves*, such as those of Pink Ice Plant (*Delosperma cooperi*), conspicuously store water in their leaves for use in dry conditions. *Small leaves*, such as those of Lead Plant (*Amorpha canescens*), are likely to be another way of maintaining lower leaf temperature. Many plants with this type of leaf also fold them, shielding them somewhat from direct exposure to the sun. *Wilting* is quite common in the leaves of many deciduous trees during very hot, sunny hours of the day, and this probably accomplishes much the same function as folding and curling of leaves.

Drought dormancy. Many plants such as Kentucky Bluegrass, Turf-type Tall Fescue, and New Mexico Privet (*Forestiera neo-mexicana*) shed their leaves and "shut down" temporarily in severe conditions.

Thorns. Arid and semiarid regions, worldwide, are noted for thorny plants. Thorns are likely to be a plant's defense against being eaten under conditions that would make it difficult to grow replacement leaves. The variety of thorns is very impressive, and this is probably a further evolutionary defense to avoid being eaten by animals that have learned to nibble around some thorns.

Fragrance. This too may be a defense against browsing by animals. Many fragrant plants, like Russian Sage (*Perovskia atriplicifolia*), are rarely, if ever, eaten by local deer.

Flavor. This seems to be still another method of discouraging browsing. In some cases, however, it appears that considerable browsing may occur before the offending creature is deterred.

Form. The *low, mounded form* of Blackfoot Daisy (*Melampodium leucanthum*) is likely to be a method of reducing exposure to excessive drying wind and sunlight. The dramatic *horizontal form* of many African Acacia trees may have evolved to reduce water loss by shading the ground. The apparent increase in leaf exposure to sunlight seems to be offset when the tiny leaflets fold during midday heat. The *rosette form* of many plants, such as Scarlet Gilia (*Gilia aggregata*) and many penstemons, makes the most of limited moisture by funneling water toward the plant.

Spacing. Creosote Bush (*Larrea tridentata*) clearly exhibits this method of avoiding competition for scarce moisture. Chemicals emitted by the roots help maintain the spacing, by making the

SURVIVING ON NO PRECIPITATION

The trade winds blowing onto the mountains of Tenerife, in the Canary Islands, support a dense cover of Broom (*Spartocytisus nubigenus*). Essentially all necessary water is obtained by condensation which falls to the soil at the base of the plants. ∎

DO BUTTERFLIES ACTUALLY LEARN?

Why should a creature that only lives for two weeks, living off flower nectar, even need to learn? The answer, according to some theories, lies in the need of flowers to get pollen to the right other flowers without wasting much of it. According to the theories, some flowers have evolved to encourage fidelity by developing distinctive shapes, colors, fragrances, and other features. All of this creates a challenge for the insects, and once they learn how to get pollen from a particular type of flower, they should seek to return to it again in order to save time and reduce vulnerability to predators while gathering nectar.

This has been tested by researchers who followed butterflies as they flitted about, and by exposing captive butterflies to one species of flower for awhile before giving them a choice of flowers. The results indicate a tendency to be faithful to a single type of flower, although there are exceptions.

Butterfly watching is certainly visually rewarding, but it also adds a little more appreciation to gardening, when some of the daily drama of butterfly life is understood. ■

area inhospitable to other plants. The effect of sandy soil on reducing available moisture is apparent by observing how thick grasslands become thin and bunchy in locations where there are scattered areas of sandier soil. This is also evident in Kentucky Bluegrass lawns where soil preparation was ignored. Both of these examples illustrate that the grasses can survive in these drier, sandier locations if they are spaced farther apart.

Dehydration/Rehydration. The cell structure and chemistry of some plants tolerate repeated cycles of dehydration and rehydration. Creosote Bush (*Larrea tridentata*), for example, is able to lose water content up to 50 percent of the dry weight of its leaves without damage. Most forest trees maintain 100 percent to 300 percent, by comparison.

Phreatophytes basically do the opposite of conserving water. They maintain active photosynthesis by drawing increasing amounts of water from permanent groundwater sources during hot, dry weather. Cottonwoods use this means of exploiting permanent sources of water in dry regions. *Xerophytes*, by contrast, make the most of arid conditions by being able to get along on soil that simply has very low moisture content. Rabbitbrush (*Chrysothamnus spp.*) is xerophytic compared with cottonwoods. *Mesophytes* are adept at functioning in moderately moist soil. Rocky Mountain Serviceberry (*Amelanchier alnifolia*) is an example of this. Some plants seem able to function in more than one capacity. Aspens (*Populus tremuloides* syn. *P. tremula*) can be found both in areas with permanently saturated subsoil and areas with much less water. In the drier situations they grow much more slowly and are likely to be quite small. Aspens, however, do appear to prefer permanently moist conditions.

Hybridization and Genetic Diversity. Rapid adaptation to local conditions through hybridization and inherent genetic diversity seems to explain the vast variability of Four-wing Saltbush (*Atriplex canescens*). Variation in Saltbush appearance alone is almost unbelievable, but it thrives in a wide variety of almost hopelessly harsh conditions, so the variability seems to serve the species well.

Ephemeral plants. This type of plant competes by growing, producing seed, and dying quickly during favorable periods. For example, introduced Eurasian Cheatgrass (*Bromus tectorum*) keeps ahead of its perennial "neighbors" by germinating in the fall, weathering winter as small plants, then developing and distributing seed in the spring, just as the native perennial grasses are getting started. Although Cheatgrass is often technically considered a winter annual, it demonstrates the advantage of a rapid and early life cycle.

Seed Survival "Strategies." *Chemical inhibitors* in some seeds serve to prevent germination in unfavorable locations and at unfavorable times. Penstemon seed, for example, is often ready for distribution in midsummer, when germination and growing conditions are not favorable. Chemical inhibitors result in improved germination of older seed and of seed exposed to various amounts of cold, damp conditions. This tends to synchronize germination with favorable spring conditions. *Tough seed coats*, like those of Wild Four O'Clock (*Mirabilis multiflora*) or Bush Morning Glory (*Ipomoea leptophylla*), presumably prevent germination before the seed has been tumbled in runoff from summer storms, or digestion by some "accommodating" bird. This may help assure wider distribution of seeds and less competition with the parent plant.

The *papery seed husks* of Paper Flower (*Psilostrophe tagetina*) appear to help with wind distribution and also appear to delay germination until thorough soaking assures greater probability of adequate moisture for initial growth. *Fire* is needed to open and release seeds of several western pine species. This appears to assure an adequate seed source when fire causes the need for major re-establishment of the species. *Massive seed production* helps assure perpetuation of plants such as Rabbitbrush (*Chrysothamnus spp.*).

The production of *succulent fruit* seems to be another means of attracting wild critters to eat the fruit and deposit the seed in places away from the parent plant. Wild Grapes (*Vitis spp.*) and Serviceberries (*Amelanchier spp.*) will germinate very poorly unless the fruit coating is thoroughly removed and thus seem to exhibit this adaptive strategy. *Spirals and coiling* are among the more amazing techniques developed by seeds to aid in successful germination. The seeds of Curl-leaf Mountain Mahogany (*Cercocarpus ledifolius*), for example, coil in damp conditions and straighten out when dry. This serves to help work the seed into the ground. *Plumes*, such as those of clematis species (*Clematis spp.*) and Apache Plume (*Fallugia paradoxa*) help with wind distribution of the seed.

It can be somewhat perplexing to notice that plants in close proximity sometimes exhibit apparently opposite adaptations to the same conditions. Shallow-rooted Cactus (*Opuntia spp.*), for example, can often be found adjacent to deep-rooted Big Western Sage (*Artemisia tridentata*). Usually, this simply illustrates that there is more than one way to cope with the conditions. It may also be a way for plants to exist in close proximity without directly competing too much.

It can be equally perplexing to notice that the same adaptive strategy is employed by plants in different environmental circumstances. Leaf hairs, for example, are useful in reducing exposure

REVIVAL FROM EXTREME DESICCATION

An extreme example of revival from extraordinary desiccation involves tissue of *Parkinsonia microphyla*, a spiny shrub or small tree. Some cells of this plant are reported to have survived after being in a continuously desiccated condition on an herbarium sheet for 250 years! ∎

to extreme sunlight, in reducing evaporative water loss, and in protecting leaves from exposure to extreme cold.

It is also very difficult to prove exactly how these adaptations help in many situations. However, imagination and creative guesswork are very helpful in discovering ways to propagate and grow many arid land plants.

Watering

Most of the methods that arid and semiarid plants use for coping with dry conditions suggest that deep, less frequent watering is more beneficial than frequent, shallow watering. However, very sandy soil and the presence of numerous newly transplanted additions to the garden point to exceptions. Spot irrigation of new transplants is usually preferable to overwatering the entire garden, because some of the established plants might be set back significantly if overwatered.

Weeding

Low watering zones tend to have far fewer "weeds" than high watering zone gardens. Avoiding regular cultivation helps too. Cultivation does get rid of some existing weeds but also encourages germination of new ones. Watering, to soften the ground, then pulling, usually with some kind of hooked weeding device, works well. Thorough weeding several times in the spring pays great dividends by almost eliminating problems later.

Fertilizing

The primary rule in fertilizing, especially in xeric zones, is *take it easy*. Most arid and semiarid plants do not need supplemental fertilizing in most soils, and it can cause problems, such as weak growth that needs support. Attention to initial soil preparation is usually all that is needed. With very sandy soil, spot applications of a balanced fertilizer may be helpful, but are rarely needed.

Deadheading

Removal of seed heads (deadheading) shortly after the flowers have finished blooming will often either extend the blooming period or result in a second period of bloom. Scarlet Bugler (*Penstemon barbatus*) often produces a second bloom if deadheaded shortly after blooming the first time. Indian Blanket (*Gaillardia aristata*) will frequently bloom continuously into the fall if seed heads are removed regularly. Chocolate Flower (*Berlandiera lyrata*), however, will bloom continuously all season without removal of any seeds. Experimentation with this is worthwhile.

Replacing and Adding Plants

Adding new plants among mature plants, especially in hot summer weather, will require special watering. The very porous soil that commercial plants are typically grown in will dry out extremely quickly, even if surrounding soil is moist. This may actually require several direct waterings each day in extreme conditions. Timing the planting for cool periods, or for spring and fall, is worth considering. It often helps to amend the soil around small transplants with organic matter. Creating watering saucers around small plants also helps, by keeping water from running off before it can soak in.

Getting Organized   A serious session in the garden is a lot more enjoyable with a little forethought. Anticipating needed tools and taking them along at the start is a good idea. It's a toss-up as to whether it is best to try to do every necessary task in one section of a garden, or to do one or two specific tasks throughout the garden. However, undertaking everything throughout an entire large garden in one session is likely to discourage even the most well-intentioned gardener and result in "terminal procrastination."

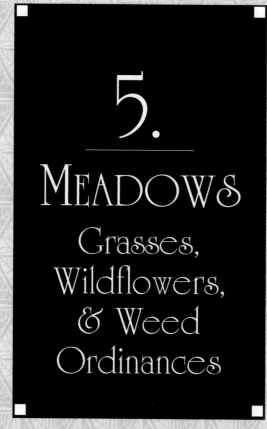

5.

MEADOWS

Grasses, Wildflowers, & Weed Ordinances

Meadows conjure up wonderful images of waving grass, pretty flowers, butterflies, and beautiful blue skies filled with fluffy little clouds. Recent meadow-mix marketing efforts certainly reinforce these images. Unfortunately, the reality of creating and maintaining meadows involves a lot more than the idyllic images portrayed on meadow-mix packaging. Even though these images may be exaggerated, an attractive, low-maintenance mix of grasses and flowers is a realistic objective and has an important role to play in waterwise landscaping. ∎

Tallgrass, Midgrass, & Shortgrass Meadows

One prerequisite for creating an attractive, permanent meadow is to have patience, because it takes time for perennial flowers and grasses to become well established. The initial rush of spectacular annual flowers in many commercial mixes is, unfortunately, a misleading prelude to the more subtle, but more rewarding perennials that can take several years to develop fully. The weather is another frequently underestimated factor. It always seems to be unusual (too dry, too hot, or too *something*), and it rarely seems to favor the gardener's optimistic expectations.

There is an infinite variety of meadows that can be created, but for gardeners in the Rocky Mountain states, a useful first step is to consider the desirable height of the meadow. The variety of predominant grasses tends to define the meadow in this respect. It is generally best to use bunch grasses, rather than spreading grasses, in order to avoid crowding out desirable wildflowers.

Many of the grasses in the following suggested mixes have the added bonus of turning beautiful shades of gold and reddish-brown in the fall, and the seeds on some are attractive through the winter. A more complete listing of plants for each meadow type is included in the Appendix.

Tallgrass meadows (approximately waist high) are typically associated with areas of greater than average moisture in the Rocky Mountain region and are probably best considered for moderate watering zones. Big Bluestem (*Andropogon gerardii*), Indiangrass (*Sorghastrum nutans*), and Switchgrass (*Panicum virgatum*) are the basic grasses of this meadow type. Wildflowers for consideration in this type of meadow include Wild White Yarrow (*Achillea lanulosa*), Purple Coneflower (*Echinacea purpurea*), and Lewis' Flax (*Linum perenne* var. *lewisii*).

Midgrass meadows (approximately knee high) are associated with slightly drier situations than tallgrass meadows. Depending on the soil and local weather, moderate to low watering zones are probably satisfactory. Little Bluestem (*Andropogon scoparius*), Sideoats Grama (*Bouteloua curtipendula*), and Asiatic Crested Wheatgrass (*Agropyron cristatum*) are good grasses for meadows of this height. Wildflowers that grow well in midgrass meadows include Wild White Yarrow (*Achillea lanulosa*), Mexican Hat Coneflower (*Ratibida columnifera*), and Purple Prairie Clover (*Dalea purpurea*).

Shortgrass meadows (approximately ankle high) require the least amount of water. In fact, even moderate watering tends to encourage mid and tall grasses to invade shortgrass meadows along the Front Range of Colorado. Low watering zone conditions are important in maintaining this type of meadow. Buffalograss

(*Buchloë dactyloides*), and Blue Grama (*Bouteloua gracilis*) are the two most common grasses in shortgrass meadows. Mexican Hat Coneflower (*Ratibida columnifera*), Snakeweed (*Gutierrezia sarothrae*), and Dotted Gayfeather (*Liatris punctata*) are good wildflowers for shortgrass meadows. Because Buffalograss is so aggressive, Blue Grama is likely to be better when wildflowers are of major interest.

Custom vs. Commercial Meadow Mixes

Most of the commercial mixes on the market are designed more to sell to a wide market than to create meadows that are well adapted to a specific situation. This leads to interest in custom mixes. The first step in making custom mixes is to determine what species to include, and the second is to determine what quantities of each species to include. To help with step one, several mixes are included in the Appendix. For the second step, consult *Southwestern Landscaping with Native Plants* by Judith Phillips (see Bibliography), which provides considerable detailed and useful information about this. Individual research with commercial seed sources and local gardeners is also recommended.

Planting a Meadow

The following information summarizes one good way to establish meadows in this region.

Planting time. Planting in March (for the Denver area) will probably satisfy the needs of those plants requiring a period of cold before germination. Planting in March or April is probably early enough to result in some flowers the first year. Planting in May through August will allow good growth the first year and good bloom the second year. Planting after August is not recommended, because inadequate growth before winter is likely to result.

Stratification. To assure first-year germination of seeds requiring a period of cold and damp (if planting after early spring), put enough 50/50 mix of perlite and sphagnum peat moss in sandwich bags to cover the seed. Dampen, but do not make soggy, then store in a refrigerator for four to six weeks.

Seed bed preparation. Start with an area that is as weed-free as possible. Till to create a soft, fine-textured condition. If the area is filled with weed seeds, till, then water, and wait for weed germination. Remove the weeds, then plant the wildflower seeds. *Do not highly enrich the soil with fresh manure or fertilizer.*

Sowing Seeds. Broadcast seeds by hand. Rake lightly to cover seed, or lightly cover seed with fine-textured topsoil.

Watering (½ inch per watering). During the first 3 weeks, water twice daily if there is no rain. For the second 3 weeks, water once daily, and for the third 3 weeks, water twice each week. After 9 weeks, water twice monthly until cold weather. During the second year, "wing it"—experiment—but be careful not to overwater, because overwatering is likely to encourage undesirable weeds.

Weeding. Weed by hand as needed. Inspect other garden areas to learn which seedlings are "weeds" and which are wildflowers. Presumably, the wildflowers will only show up where they were planted.

Tips to Consider. Adding pre-grown wildflower plants can significantly speed up the time needed to get blooms in a meadow. These plants can be grown at home (see "Growing Your Own Plants" in Chapter 3), or they can be purchased. Planting in sizable groups will yield the showiest visual effect. In large areas, it may be best to concentrate the wildflower seeding in specific patches. This will limit the areas needing the most attention and may result in more noticeable visual effects.

Meadow Maintenance

Managing a meadow is largely a matter of "playing it by ear." Watering, mowing (which mimics the effects of wildlife browsing and wild fires), and weeding by hand are the main activities to consider after a meadow is mature. Because the climate is drier in the Rocky Mountain region than in the midwestern prairie country, woody shrubs and trees only rarely invade meadows here. This eliminates much of the need for both mowing and burning. In fact, many meadows get along with little or no attention for years. Most meadow maintenance is really a matter of personal preference or managing to get along with the neighbors.

Weed Ordinances

Meadows are not for "neatniks," and cause difficulty in "neatnik neighborhoods." They challenge established standards and are often unwelcome. Midgrass and tallgrass meadows are especially likely to draw attention; in fact, many weed ordinances are based on mowing height. Headlines from local newspapers tell the tale: "Pulling weeds a pain, now it could be the law," "Aurora [Colorado] may triple fine for violating weed code," and "Are neat yards part of the puritan ethic?"

Actually, there are plenty of examples of marvelous meadows in very traditional neighborhoods. Part of the answer lies in managing the edges carefully. Confining tallgrass and midgrass meadows between sidewalks and driveways may help. Shortgrass meadows are more readily accepted in established suburban areas, and in more rural areas, mowing a strip around the edge or along a country road often eliminates complaints.

Many anticipated meadow problems are imaginary, but there are a few real problems to deal with. Invasive behavior is not a problem with carefully selected plants, although the neighbors may not believe it until they can see it for themselves. Misguided and misenforced local weed ordinances can be very real problems. In most communities, such codes are enforced on a case-by-case (or complaint only) basis. This allows opportunities for modifying the design, as well as talking things over with the neighbors. In some communities, however, strict fines are automatically levied: $150 per acre in Aurora, Colorado, in 1989, and involuntary mowing at $35 to $40 per hour in St. Louis, Missouri. Height limits vary in various places, with seven, eight, and twelve inches being common figures. Denver ordinances exempt edible plants (including dandelions!)

6.

CRITTERS IN THE WATERWISE GARDEN

For a lot of people, landscaping with wildlife immediately brings to mind hummingbirds and butterflies in the garden. For others, it instantly brings to mind skunks, squirrels, and raccoons rummaging in the rubbish. Because it involves both attracting wildlife and managing critter control, this subject is clearly made for controversy. For clever gardeners, however, gardening with wildlife is highly rewarding. ∎

WATERWISE WILDLIFE GARDENING PRINCIPLES

1. Be specific when planning and designing
2. Provide basic wildlife needs consistently
3. Provide wildlife nuisance control
4. Be creative and be persistent
5. Develop curiosity, appreciation, and respect for wildlife ■

 To some degree, waterwise flower gardening, as it has been described in this book, automatically invites many marvelous creatures. Butterflies and hummingbirds, for example, find some of the prettiest flowers irresistible. In fact, hummingbirds have recently been reported commuting from the foothills west of Denver to the east-side suburbs for Scarlet Hedgenettle (*Stachys coccinea*).

Control of deer damage is another almost automatic bonus of waterwise gardening. Creeping Mahonia (*Mahonia repens*) and many other moderate and low watering zone plants are rarely eaten if not overwatered. Conversely, overwatering and over-fertilizing the same plants actually appear to encourage browsing.

Although many wonderful wildlife benefits are serendipitous with waterwise gardening practices, the following principles help make the most of this experience.

1. Be Specific When Planning & Designing

Much wildlife garden writing is geographically too general to be very helpful when planning a specific yard. For example, Mountain Ash (*Sorbus spp.*) are often described as wonderful trees for birds, but in the Denver area, Mountain Ash trees are often ignored by birds. Various hawthorns (*Crataegus spp.*) and crab-apples (*Malus spp.*) are usually satisfactory substitutes. There are rich rewards in being as specific as possible, and incorporating as much local lore as possible, when applying any wildlife gardening principle.

Consider the assets and limitations of your site. How far away is the nearest natural habitat such as a stream corridor, foothills, or a lake? Even in the middle of Boulder, Colorado, goldfish have disappeared from backyard ponds—victims of neighborhood king-fishers. Also, rock wrens and marmots inhabit a rock garden at the Denver Botanic Gardens in central Denver. So, urban areas have great potential, but proximity to natural areas will increase the odds of success and will offer a good idea about which species are likely to visit the wildlife garden.

List the wildlife species you *do* want to attract. This is the place to begin detailed planning. With a good list of species to attract, the selection and arrangement of plants, bird houses, and feeders becomes a lot of fun, and the chances of success are far better than taking "potluck" at the first garden center and hoping for the best. See the Appendix for detailed lists of plants for various wildlife species.

List the species that you *do not* want to attract. This is just as important as listing what you *do* want. Deer, for example, are becoming an everyday occurrence in many areas, especially in foothill locations. If this is known in advance, plants can be

RUSSIAN OLIVE PROBLEMS

Although the seeds of Russian Olive trees (*Elaeagnus angustifolia*) are phenomenally popular with an array of wildlife species, these trees have become a serious invasive problem in many Rocky Mountain flood plain areas. This has prompted a growing opinion that they should not be used (even occasionally) as landscape plants. Various hawthorns (*Crataegus spp.*) and crabapples (*Malus spp.*) make suitable substitutes. ■

Feeders are an excellent way to help wildlife span time periods when natural food supplies are low. Careful attention to the exact food used will be well rewarded. This case illustrates the popularity of water and ordinary table sugar (in a 4:1 ratio). *Photo by John Dudley.*

Purple Coneflower (*Echinacea purpurea*) is a good butterfly plant for moderate watering zones.

Pitcher Sage (*Salvia pitcheri*) is an excellent plant for xeric zones. Its blue flowers are a delightful addition to late summer and early fall gardens, and it attracts many monarch butterflies.

A praying mantis is an intriguing addition to wildlife gardens and illustrates that urban wildlife consists of much more than songbirds, squirrels, and occasional raccoons.

Hawkmoths can very frequently be seen visiting Double Bubble Mint (*Agastache cana*), where they sometimes must compete with hummingbirds for sips of Double Bubble Mint ambrosia.

Raccoons can be a real nuisance, but with some imagination and persistence, it is often possible to keep them out of raspberry patches and fruit trees and thus enjoy their cleverness and each spring's cute little raccoons.

It is very interesting to wonder about what wild creatures see when they travel about during their daily lives. The swallowtail butterfly may visually blend with the Daylily petals and be essentially invisible to prospective predators who may lack the color discrimination that humans have.

A carefully reconstructed shortgrass prairie at the Denver Botanic Gardens, as it typically appears in late June. Plants include Buffalograss (*Buchloë dactyloides*), Blue Grama (*Bouteloua gracilis*), Mexican Hat Coneflower (*Ratibida columnifera*), (*Yucca glauca*), and Fringed Sage (*Artemisia frigida*).

A midgrass prairie at the base of the foothills in Boulder, Colorado, as it typically appears in late summer and early fall. Western Wheatgrass (*Agropyron smithii*), Sideoats Grama (*Bouteloua curtipendula*), and Little Bluestem (*Andropogon scoparius*) are the dominant grasses.

A tallgrass prairie reconstructed at the Denver Botanic Gardens in October. Grass species include Indiangrass (*Sorghastrum nutans*), Big Bluestem (*Andropogon gerardii*), and Switchgrass (*Panicum virgatum*).

Low watering zone flowers can provide continual color from spring through fall. Visual interest can be extended through the winter season with a few selected shrubs, in this case Green Ephedra (*Ephedra viridis*), Piñon Pine (*Pinus edulis*), and Soaptree Yucca (*Yucca elata*).

▲ June flowers include:
Scarlet Bugler Penstemon (*P. barbatus*), Late Easter Daisy (*Townsendia grandiflora*), Cobaea Penstemon (*P. cobaea*), Chocolate Flower (*Berlandiera lyrata*), Showy Goldeneye (*Viguiera multiflora*), and Lewis' Flax (*Linum perenne* var. *lewisii*).

Edible landscaping can be extremely attractive. The intense blue of the Borage (*Borago officinalis*) makes a spectacular focal feature when viewed through the foreground grape arbor. ▶

▲ July flowers include:
Showy Goldeneye (*Viguiera multiflora*), Purple Cone Flower (*Echinacea purpurea*), Paper Flower (*Psilostrophe tagetina*), Indian Pink (*Silene laciniata*), *Penstemon kunthii*, Lewis' Flax (*Linum perenne* var. *lewisii*), and Chocolate Flower (*Berlandiera lyrata*).

September flowers include:
Showy Goldeneye (*Viguiera multiflora*), Chocolate Flower (*Berlandiera lyrata*), Pitcher Sage (*Salvia pitcheri*), Double Bubble Mint (*Agastache cana*), Scarlet Hedgenettle (*Stachys coccinea*), California Zauschneri (*Zauschneri californica*), Mexican Hat Coneflower (*Ratibida columnifera*), and Broom Groundsel (*Senecio spartioides*).

NEVADA GARDEN HUMMINGBIRDS

Reports from the Reno area of Nevada indicate that at various times during the year, gardeners can reasonably expect to attract four species of hummingbirds: rufous, black-chinned, broad-tailed, and calliope. ■

selected to discourage damage. There is a lot that can be done to attract some critters while discouraging others. See the Appendix for a list of deer-resistant plants.

Identify beneficial plant and animal associations to be encouraged. Mutualism (cooperative relationships in which all participants benefit) is a fascinating theme to plan into gardens. Growing melons in a cold frame is a good way to demonstrate the mutualistic value of bee pollination. Melons want warmer conditions than exist in many Rocky Mountain gardens. In a cold frame, they often do much better. Pollination is a problem, however, unless the top is propped open at the right time. This demonstrates the melons' need for bees and also meets the bees' need for pollen to manufacture honey. *Homo sapiens* benefits from both by making it all possible in an unnatural location. Predator/prey relationships can work to the clever gardener's advantage. Consider Big Western Sagebrush (*Artemisia tridentata*). Almost every year along the Colorado Front Range, little black aphids have appeared on these fragrant shrubs in early spring. When there has been enough warm weather, ladybugs, then ladybug larvae, appear and completely eliminate the aphids within a few days—no pesticides needed and no harm done to the sagebrush.

2. Provide Basic Wildlife Needs Consistently

Consistency in providing the following basic wildlife needs is just as important as meeting each specific basic wildlife need.

Food. Paying attention to specific foods for specific wildlife species and knowing what works well in your particular area are the keys to success. Hummingbirds are a good example. In Colorado, they usually arrive in late April and leave in early September. In cities along the Colorado Front Range, they can be attracted throughout the entire season with early penstemons such as Scarlet Bugler (*Penstemon barbatus*), midseason penstemons like Murray's Penstemon (*Penstemon murrayanus*), or Scarlet Hedgenettle (*Stachys coccinea*), and late in the season with Double Bubble Mint (*Agastache cana*). Feeders can help span gaps in the flower sequence.

Hummingbird behavior in the Rocky Mountain region is likely to vary considerably in different localities. In Santa Fe, Albuquerque, and Flagstaff, for example, Zauschneria (*Zauschneria californica*) is likely to be a very good hummingbird plant during October. In northern and central Colorado, however, this plant is likely to be a poor choice because the birds move south about the time Zauschneria begins to bloom. Double Bubble Mint would probably be a good late-blooming plant for hummingbirds in all of these areas. In Spokane, it may be possible to attract the aggressive rufous hummingbird with *Penstemon murrayanus* and *P. kunthii*,

SKUNK CONTROL

If skunks become a problem, under a deck for example, they can frequently be encouraged to move along to a more suitable (to humans) location by placing moth balls in the area they are not wanted. It has been suggested that it is possible to determine if the skunks are still inhabiting the location by sprinkling flour near the suspected entrance. White footprints supposedly will give away the presence of the creatures, but if they are not "smellable" any more, why bother with the flour? ∎

since this hummingbird nests in that northerly area at the time these penstemons would probably be in bloom. Discovering what works well in each locality is one of the interesting undertakings in wildlife gardening. See Appendix for various wildlife plant lists.

Water. Even a simple birdbath can be a very dramatic addition to a flower garden. A consistent water supply is important, and dripping water attracts even more species than still water. Location is important too. Consider sun vs. shade and open vs. sheltered areas. Experimentation with these variables is valuable.

Shelter. This includes such common and uncommon items as birdhouses, butterfly shelters, and bat boxes. Some of these can be very ornamental. However, it is important to pay special attention to specific real needs of the species involved. The wildlife section of the bibliography (see Appendix) includes sources of additional information about this.

Habitat diversity. Simply arranging the landscape into different watering zones accomplishes a lot of diversity. Also, by adding more flowering plants to the typical landscape, many more species will find what they need. In general, the greater the diversity of the landscape, the greater the variety of wildlife that will be interested in the landscape.

Effective habitat arrangement. The location of various elements in the wildlife landscape can be a key to success. For example, if a bird feeder does not attract birds in one location, try another. A new location, only a few feet away, sometimes attracts many more birds. The same birdhouse located at different heights is likely to attract different birds. With this in mind, it would be worthwhile to mount houses of the same design at different levels on the same tree, because chickadees are likely to use a house that is farther off the ground than one that wrens would use.

Consistent year-round provisions. There are critical times when it is especially important to provide reliable sources of food, water, and shelter. A "hit-or-miss" approach to providing essential wildlife needs is a common source of disappointment in wildlife gardening. Allowing a few "weeds" (such as mullein or thistle) to go to seed can be worth the risk of a few unwanted seedlings in the spring. Mullein will sometimes attract chickadees and downy woodpeckers, while thistles will sometimes attract goldfinches to the garden. Attention to specific feeder foods (such as thistle for finches and sugar water for hummingbirds) can help a lot in bridging gaps in natural food supply.

Keeping birdbaths full of water in dry periods is worth special attention, because the local critters will soon learn to visit a water source they can depend on in difficult, dry times.

Protection from danger. Fencing out neighborhood dogs may be necessary. Providing open areas on the ground, near bird feeders and birdbaths, sometimes provides significant protection from neighborhood cats. Mothballs placed in plastic sandwich bags among hummingbird plants may discourage family cats from hanging out and springing on unsuspecting hummers. The cats actually destroy many more plants than they kill hummingbirds. Cats can't change direction once they're off the ground, but hummingbirds specialize in this. Ribbon streamers near windows and hawk silhouettes on the glass may help to deter birds from crashing into windows.

Avoiding the use of pesticides and herbicides is critical to the creation of successful butterfly gardens, and the wide variety of environmentally acceptable remedies available in local garden centers offers just about everything any gardener will need.

3. Provide Wildlife Nuisance Control

There are plenty of clever and troublesome critters to contend with in the wildlife yard. But, when it comes to "questionable" wildlife, remember that they are part of the grand scheme of things, too, and may be much more beneficial than one may appreciate at first.

Deer offer a good example of the benefits of tolerance training and appreciation adaptation. If we can't change the deer, maybe we can change our gardens and our attitudes instead. Accepting the challenge and applying some ingenuity usually makes it possible to have the plants and the deer also.

Fences of black plastic netting, available at most garden stores, work wonders in reducing browsing! Deer could easily rip it down, but rarely (if ever) do. It's amazing! Netting is much easier to work with than chicken wire, and is almost invisible from a distance.

Though deer sooner or later try almost any plant they encounter, there are a few plants that seem to be relatively immune from severe devastation. These include daffodils, iris, yarrow, Creeping Mahonia (*Mahonia repens*), Piñon Pine, and Colorado Spruce. See Appendix for a detailed list of these plants. In addition, plants that are grown without irrigation are often browsed less than highly watered plants.

Some plants apparently repel deer by virtue of their fragrance, while others repel them by taste. Still others seem to combine both strategies. Artificial repellents work on the same principles. The most effective rely on fragrance, because this tends to keep the deer from trying a plant before deciding whether to go for more. To make matters even more interesting, deer vary somewhat in their preferences. Who knows, some may even have allergies so that fragrance doesn't matter much?

DUMPSTER-SIZE RACCOON REPORTED

Raccoons can be cute, but consider the mischief potential of the largest raccoon on record. It was killed in Wisconsin in 1955, and measured 55 inches from tongue to tail and weighed 62 pounds 6 ounces! ■

In spite of the complexities, the repellent "Deer Away" has completely kept deer from eating many of their traditionally favorite plants, such as tulips, crocus, and roses. This repellent is based on the smell of rotten eggs, but at levels too low for gardeners to detect.

Another repellent, "Ropel," is not only reported to keep cats out from under bird feeders but is also reported to discourage flickers from pounding and pecking at houses. There are also reports that this repellent, as well as epsom salts, effectively deter rabbits.

With butterflies, remember that they are not only beautiful, they are also important pollinators. They are caterpillars, however, in their "other" lives, though most don't really do much damage. Tolerance is in order when encountering caterpillars in the wildlife garden.

4. Be Creative & Be Persistent

Problems often become opportunities in the wildlife garden, and it is very possible to enjoy skunks, squirrels, and raccoons when you've learned a few tricks for getting along with them. Imagination and persistence appear to be potent forms of magic, after discovering that deer don't like daffodils but will devour nearby roses, or that raccoons won't bother a raspberry patch with mothballs in plastic bags scattered in it. Mothballs have also worked to protect fruit in fruit trees.

Be persistent when trying to get along with critters in your garden. Remember, they never quit! Although you may win for awhile, it's never forever. So try to enjoy the game.

5. Develop Curiosity, Appreciation, & Respect for Wildlife

Try to visualize the world as the critters see it. Learn about the special vision of bees, birds, cats, and insects. Photographing wildlife in the garden teaches you to see things that would otherwise be missed. Drawing, like photography, sharpens the gardener's powers of observation in its own way. Become a nature detective and be alert to the clues about what happens in the garden when you are not there.

Waterwise gardening for wildlife is a complex subject, but those willing to get involved will be rewarded when their ordinary landscapes are transformed into delightful, easily maintained gardens full of mystery and magic.

Amazing Hummingbirds

- It has been said that if a 170-pound human had a metabolic rate as high as the average hummingbird, he would have to eat about twice his weight in food daily, and his body temperature would be over 750°F. Likewise, to correspond to the calorie consumption of an

HUMMINGBIRDS IN KANSAS

Two species of humming-birds occur in Kansas—ruby-throated and rufous. The ruby-throated hum-mingbirds occur through-out the state, usually nesting along streams. They are most common, however, in the eastern half of the state. The rufous hummingbird is sometimes seen in west-ern Kansas on its south-ward migration in late summer. This aggressive little bird has been re-ferred to as the "darting atom of bird life" by one Kansas observer, while in Arizona it has been nick-named the Red Baron. ■

average hummingbird, a 170-pound human would have to consume about 370 pounds of potatoes, or 285 pounds of hamburger.

- Both the amount of nectar and the sugar content of the nectar in flowers varies considerably, and this may explain the reason hum-mingbirds stay much longer at some flowers than at others. Indian Pink (*Silene laciniata*) is an example of a good waterwise flower that hummers tend to visit for remarkably long periods.
- In order of their preference, hummingbirds like sucrose, glucose, and finally fructose. Studies show that many of the commercial feeder foods are actually rejected by the birds, and the current recommenda-tion is to mix water with ordinary table sugar in a 4:1 ratio. *Honey should be avoided.*
- An average hummingbird is reported to pass 75 to 85 percent of its body weight in water daily. This would be equivalent to an adult human passing 20 gallons of water daily.
- Hummingbirds also eat considerable numbers of insects, and studies indicate that it takes only ten minutes for the unused parts of an insect to pass completely through a hummingbird.
- Some of the remarkable little rufous hummingbirds complete an annual migration journey of more than 4,000 miles, each way, between Central America and Alaska. There are also reports that ruby-throated hummingbirds sometimes cross the Gulf of Mexico in 20 hours—a non-stop 500-mile journey.

Based on the following adaptations of many flowers, hummingbird pol-lination would seem to be very valuable, while pollination by insects would appear to be a problem.

- Many flowers are red, which birds see well but most insects apparently see poorly.
- Some flowers hang downward making it difficult, or impossible, for many insects to enter the flower.
- Some flowers have back-turned petals, which discourage insects from getting into the flower.
- The bases of some tubular flowers are thickened, discouraging insects from breaking into the flower for nectar.
- Many hummingbird-pollinated flowers have no fragrance, apparently to discourage insects (which often use fragrance to locate flowers). Hummingbirds probably have no sense of smell, so this is likely to be irrelevant in their finding the flowers.
- Some flowers have grooves that guide the birds' beaks into the flower, and have their reproductive parts located deep in the flower tubes to reduce chances of being damaged by the birds' beaks.

The reasons for all of this remain largely a mystery. It does appear, how-ever, that hawkmoths are an important insect exception, possibly ac-complishing more pollination of certain flowers than hummingbirds. It has even been suggested that the flowers evolved in response to the moths rather than the hummingbirds. ■

7.

Waterwise Plant Lists & Profiles

❀ Time-Tested Plants
    Herbaceous Flowers
    Deciduous Shrubs
    Evergreen Shrubs
    Ornamental Grasses

❀ Plants with Great Waterwise Potential
    Herbaceous Flowers
    Shrubs

❀ Plant Profiles
    Herbaceous Flowers
    Deciduous Shrubs
    Evergreen Shrubs
    Ornamental Grasses

Time-Tested Plants

The water requirements of these plants have been observed in a wide variety of conditions, over several years, in the Denver-Boulder area.

Waterwise Watering Zones

The primary purpose of developing the watering zones indicated in these lists is to aid the gardener in grouping together plants of similar water needs. These groups should remain constant even though differences in altitude, latitude, and soil type are likely to require adjustments in the precise amounts of water needed in a specific garden. The amounts of water indicated (in inches per week) refer to typical Denver midsummer irrigation needs for periods without rain. The figures (in gallons of water per square foot) refer to irrigation needed for a typical 20-week irrigation season. The area of native origin is indicated in order to offer additional information about conditions to which the plants are best suited.

High Watering Zones:	Moderate Watering Zones:	Low Watering Zones:
■ 18-20 gals. added per sq. ft. per 20-week season	■ 10± gals. added per sq. ft. per 20-week season	■ 0 to 3 gals. added per sq. ft. per 20-week season
■ .5″ added 3 times per week	■ .75″ added once per week	■ .5″ added every other week
■ Approx. 30″ added over 20 wks.	■ Approx. 16″ added over 20 wks.	■ Approx. 4.5″ added over 20 wks.
Typical plants: Kentucky Bluegrass lawns, Redtwig Dogwood, Pansies	*Typical plants: Turf-type Tall Fescue lawns, Potentilla, Purple Coneflower*	*Typical plants: Buffalograss lawns, Rabbitbrush, Mexican Hat Coneflower*

KEY TO PLANT LIST SYMBOLS

☘ = Plants with detailed descriptions
H = High watering zone
M = Moderate watering zone
L = Low watering zone
N = Native to the Rocky Mountain region
FS = Full sun
PS = Part sun
SH = Shade
± = An ability to survive in conditions somewhat more or less than a single category

HERBACEOUS FLOWERS

Botanic Name	Familiar Name	Water Zone	Light	Native Origin
Abronia fragrans	Sand Verbena	L	FS	N
Achillea ageratifolia	Greek Yarrow	L,M	FS	Greece
Achillea × 'Coronation Gold'	Coronation Gold Yarrow	L,M	FS	Hybrid
Achillea filipendulina	Fernleaf Yarrow	L,M	FS	Asia M., Cauc.
❀ *Achillea lanulosa*	Native White Yarrow	M±	FS	N
Achillea millefolium	Common Yarrow	M±	FS	Europe
Achillea millefolium 'Summer Pastels'	Summer Pastels Yarrow	M±	FS	Cultivar
Achillea × 'Moonshine'	Moonshine Yarrow	L,M	FS	Hybrid
Achillea tomentosa	Woolly Yarrow	L,M	FS	Eur. to w. Asia
❀ *Agastache cana*	Double Bubble Mint	L,M	FS	N.M., w. Tex.
Antennaria spp.	Pussy-toes	L,M	FS	N
Aquilegia caerulea	Native Blue Columbine	H,M	PS±	N
Aquilegia chrysantha	Native Yellow Columbine	H,M	PS±	N
Aquilegia elegantula	Native Red Columbine	H,M	PS±	N
Asclepias tuberosa	Butterfly Weed	L,M	FS	N
Aster bigelovii (syn. *Machaeranthera bigelovii*)	Santa Fe Aster	L	FS	N
Aster porteri	Porter's Aster	L	FS	N
Aurinia saxatilis	Basket-of-gold	L,M	FS	S.c. Eur., Turk.
❀ *Berlandiera lyrata*	Chocolate Flower	L	FS	N
❀ *Callirhoe involucrata*	Poppy Mallow	L	FS	N
Campanula rotundifolia	Harebell	L,M	PS±	N
❀ *Centranthus ruber*	Red Valerian	L,M	FS	Medit. region
Cerastium tomentosum	Snow-in-summer	L,M	FS	Mtns. of Italy
Chrysanthemum leucanthemum	Ox-eye Daisy	L,M	FS,PS	Eurasia
Chrysanthemum × superbum	Shasta Daisy	M±	FS	Hybrid
Chrysopsis fulcrata (syn. *Heterotheca fulcrata*)	Golden Aster	L,M	FS	N
Chrysopsis villosa (syn. *Heterotheca villosa*)	Golden Aster	L,M	FS	N
Coreopsis grandiflora	Tickseed	L,M	FS	Eastern U.S.
❀ *Coreopsis lanceolata*	Lanceleaf Coreopsis	L,M	FS	Eastern U.S.
Crocus spp.	Crocus species	L,M	FS	Medit., c. Asia
Dalea purpurea (syn. *Petalostemon purpurea*)	Purple Prairie Clover	L,M	FS	N
❀ *Delosperma cooperi*	Hardy Pink Ice Plant	L,M	FS	Southern Africa
Delosperma nubigenum (*congestum?*)	Hardy Yellow Ice Plant	L,M	FS	Southern Africa
❀ *Digitalis lanata*	Grecian Foxglove	L,M	FS,PS	S. Eur. to n. Chi.

Botanic Name	Familiar Name	Water Zone	Light	Native Origin
✤ Echinacea purpurea	Purple Coneflower	M±	FS,PS	N
Epilobium angustifolium	Fireweed	M,H	FS,PS	N. Amer., Euras.
Eriogonum umbellatum	Sulphur Flower	L	FS,PS	N
Eschscholzia californica	California Poppy	L,M	FS	Calif.
Euphorbia myrsinites	Myrtle Euphorbia	L	FS	Europe
✤ Eustoma grandiflorum	Tulip Gentian	M,H	FS	N
Gaillardia aristata	Gaillardia, Indian Blanket	M±	FS	N
Geranium caespitosum	Native Hardy Geranium	M±	FS,PS,SH	N
Geranium pratense × himalayense 'Johnson's Blue'	Johnson's Blue Geranium	M±	PS±	Eurasia
Geranium sanguineum	Bloodred Geranium	M±	PS±	Eurasia
✤ Gilia aggregata (syn. Ipomopsis aggregata)	Scarlet Gilia	L,M	FS	N
Goniolimon tataricum	Tartar Statice	L,M	FS	Medit. to c. Asia
✤ Gutierrezia sarothrae	Snakeweed	L	FS	N
Gypsophila pacifica	Baby's Breath	L,M	FS	C. Asia to Manch.
Gypsophila paniculata	Baby's Breath	L,M	FS	C. Europe to C. Asia
Gypsophila repens	Creeping Baby's Breath	L,M	FS	S. Europe
✤ Helianthus maximiliani	Maximilian's Sunflower	M±	FS	N
Hemerocallis spp. and hybrids	Daylilies	M±	FS,PS	Eastern Asia
Iris (bearded hybrids)	Bearded Iris sp. and var.	L,M	FS	Hybrid
Iris danfordiae	Danford Iris	L,M	FS	E. Turkey
Iris reticulata	Violet-scented Iris	L,M	FS	Turkey
Iris spp. (Central Asian species)	Central Asian Iris	L,M	FS	C. Asia
Iris bucharica	—	L,M	FS	
Iris × 'Dushanbe'	—	L,M	FS	
Iris hoogiana	—	L,M	FS	
Iris kolpakowskiana	—	L,M	FS	
Iris magnifica	—	L,M	FS	
Iris willmottiana	—	L,M	FS	
Kniphofia spp.	Poker Plants	M±	FS	Africa
Lavandula angustifolia	English lavender	M±	FS,PS	Medit. region
Leucocrinum montanum	Sandlily	L,M	FS	N
✤ Liatris punctata	Dotted Gayfeather	L	FS	N
Limonium latifolium	Sea Lavender	M±	FS	Rum., Bulg., S. Russia
✤ Linum perenne var. lewisii	Lewis' Flax	M±	FS,PS	N
Lychnis coronaria	Rose Campion	L,M	FS,PS	Medit. to c. Asia

Botanic Name	Familiar Name	Water Zone	Light	Native Origin
❀ Melampodium leucanthum	Blackfoot Daisy	L	FS	N
❀ Mirabilis multiflora	Wild Four O'Clock	L	FS,PS	N
Monarda didyma 'Cambridge Scarlet'	Cambridge Scarlet	H	PS±	E. North Amer.
❀ Monarda fistulosa	Wild Monarda	M,H	PS±	N
Narcissus spp.	Daffodils	L,M,H		Medit. region
❀ Oenothera caespitosa	White-tufted Evening Primrose	L	FS	N
Oenothera missouriensis	Ozark Evening Primrose	L,M	FS	N
Oxytropis lambertii	Lambert's Locoweed	L	FS	N
Paeonia spp.	Peonies	M±	FS,PS	Eurasia
❀ Penstemon alpinus	Alpine Penstemon	L,M	FS	N
Penstemon ambiguus	Sand Penstemon	L	FS	N
Penstemon angustifolius	Narrowleaf Penstemon	L,M	FS	Great Plains
❀ Penstemon barbatus	Scarlet Bugler	L,M	FS	N
❀ Penstemon barbatus 'Schooley's Yellow'	Schooley's Yellow Penstemon	L,M	FS	Cultivar
❀ Penstemon cobaea	Cobaea Penstemon	L,M	FS	N
Penstemon crandallii	Crandall's Penstemon	L,M	FS	Colo.
Penstemon cyananthus	Wasatch Penstemon	L,M	FS	N
❀ Penstemon digitalis 'Husker Red'	Husker Red Penstemon	L,M	FS,PS	Great Plains
Penstemon eatonii	Eaton's Penstemon	L,M	FS	S. Calif., Ariz.
Penstemon gormanii	Gorman's Penstemon	L,M	FS	Alaska
Penstemon grandiflorus 'Albus'	White Wild Snapdragon	L,M	FS	N
❀ Penstemon kunthii	Kunthii Penstemon	L,M	FS	North Mex.
Penstemon linarioides	Mat Penstemon	L,M	FS	Ariz., New Mex.
❀ Penstemon murrayanus	Murray's Penstemon	L,M	FS	E. Tex., Okla.
Penstemon neo-mexicanus	New Mexico Penstemon	L,M	FS	N
❀ Penstemon pinifolius	Pineleaf Penstemon	L,M	FS	S. Ariz., New Mex., Mex.
❀ Penstemon pseudospectabilis	Showy Penstemon	L,M	FS	Calif. deserts, Ariz.
Penstemon richardsonii	Richardson's Penstemon	L,M	FS	Pac. n.w., east of mtns.
Penstemon secundiflorus	Sidebells Penstemon	L,M	FS	N
❀ Penstemon strictus	Rocky Mountain Penstemon	L,M	FS	N
Penstemon virens	Bluemist Penstemon	L,M	FS,PS	N
❀ Perovskia atriplicifolia	Russian Sage	M±	FS	Central Asia
Phlox nana	Santa Fe Phlox	L	FS	New Mex., Ariz., Tex., Mex.
Phlox subulata	Creeping Phlox	L,M	FS	N.east U.S.
Psilostrophe bakeri	Paperflower	L	FS	N

	Botanic Name	Familiar Name	Water Zone	Light	Native Origin
❀	*Psilostrophe tagetina*	Paperflower	L	FS	N
	Pulsatilla spp.	Pasque Flowers	L,M	FS	N. Amer., Euras.
❀	*Ratibida columnifera*	Mexican Hat Coneflower	L	FS	N
	Rosa spp.	Roses	M±	FS	World-wide
	Rudbeckia fulgida 'Goldsturm'	Goldsturm Gloriosa Daisy	M	FS	E. North Amer.
	Rudbeckia hirta	Gloriosa Daisy	M±	FS	E. North Amer.
	Salvia officinalis	Cooking Sage	L,M	FS	Medit. region
❀	*Salvia pitcheri*	Pitcher Sage	L	FS	N
	(syn. *Salvia azurea* var. *grandiflora*)				
	Santolina chamaecyparissus	Santolina	L,M	FS	Medit. region
	Saponaria ocymoides	Rock Soapwort	M±	FS,PS	S. Europe
	Sedum spp.	Sedum species	M±	FS	North Amer.
❀	*Senecio longilobus*	Threadleaf Groundsel	L	FS	N
	Senecio spartioides	Broom Groundsel	L	FS	N
❀	*Silene laciniata*	Indian Pink,			
		Mexican Campion	L	FS	N
	Solidago spp.	Goldenrods	L,M,H	FS	Mostly N. Amer.
	Sphaeralcea spp.	Globemallows	L	FS	N
	Stachys byzantina	Lamb's Ears	L,M	FS	S.w. Asia
❀	*Stachys coccinea*	Scarlet Hedgenettle	M±	FS,PS	N
	Stanleya pinnata	Prince's Plume	L	FS	N
	Talinum calycinum	Fame Flower	L,M	FS	N
	Thermopsis spp.	Goldenbanner	M±	FS	N
	Thymus spp.	Thyme species	L,M	FS	Europe
	Tulipa spp. (Central Asian species)	Central Asian Wild Tulips	L,M	FS	C. Asia
	Tulipa batalinii	—	L,M	FS	
	Tulipa clusiana	—	L,M	FS	
	Tulipa greigii	—	L,M	FS	
	Tulipa kaufmanniana	—	L,M	FS	
	Tulipa kolpakowskiana	—	L,M	FS	
	Tulipa maximoviczii	—	L,M	FS	
	Tulipa praestans	—	L,M	FS	
	Tulipa tarda				
	(syn. *Tulipa dasystemon*)	—	L,M	FS	
	Tulipa turkestanica	—	L,M	FS	
❀	*Verbena bipinnatifida*	Dakota Verbena	L	FS	N
❀	*Viguiera multiflora*	Showy Goldeneye	L,M	FS	N
	Viola nutallii	Nutall's Violet	L,M	FS	N
	Viola pedatifida	Birdfoot Violet	L,M	FS	N
❀	*Zauschneria californica*	California Zauschneria	L,M	FS	Calif.
❀	*Zinnia grandiflora*	Prairie Zinnia	L	FS	N

DECIDUOUS SHRUBS

The following shrubs fit well with waterwise flower gardens. Most are small to medium in size, some have showy flowers, others have colorful foliage or stems, and all will add interest during the winter, when most of the flowers have died back to the ground.

Botanic Name	Familiar Name	Water Zone	Light	Native Origin
✿ *Amorpha canescens*	Leadplant	L,M	FS	N
Amorpha nana	Dwarf Leadplant	L,M	FS	N
Buddleia alternifolia	Butterfly Bush	L	FS	N.w. China
Buddleia davidii	Butterfly Bush	M±	FS	China
Caryopteris × *clandonensis*	Bluemist Spirea	L,M	FS	Orient
✿ *Chamaebatiaria millefolium*	Fernbush	L	FS	N
✿ *Chrysothamnus spp.*	Rabbitbrush species	L	FS	N
Euonymus alata 'Compacta'	Dwarf Burning Bush	M±	FS,PS,SH	Orient
✿ *Fallugia paradoxa*	Apache Plume	L	FS	N
Forestiera neomexicana	New Mexico Privet	M±	FS	N
Hibiscus syriacus	Rose of Sharon Hibiscus	M±	FS	Asia
Hippophae rhamnoides	Sea Buckthorn	M±	FS	Eurasia
Holodiscus dumosus	Rock Spirea	M±	FS,PS	N
Jamesia americana	Jamesia, Waxflower	M,H	PS,SH	N
✿ *Rosa glauca* (syn. *Rosa rubrifolia*)	Redleaf Rose	M±	FS,PS,SH	C. Eur. mtns.

EVERGREEN SHRUBS

Botanic Name	Familiar Name	Water Zone	Light	Native Origin
❀ *Artemisia tridentata*	Big Western Sage	L,M	FS	N
Cercocarpus intricatus	Little-leaf Mountain Mahogany	L	FS	N
❀ *Cowania mexicana*	Cowania	L	FS	N
❀ *Ephedra nevadensis*	Nevada Ephedra	L,M	FS	N
❀ *Ephedra torreyana*	Torrey Ephedra	L,M	FS	N
❀ *Ephedra viridis*	Green Ephedra	L,M	FS	N
❀ *Mahonia fremontii*	Fremont Mahonia	L,M	FS,PS	N
❀ *Mahonia haematocarpa*	Redberry Mahonia	L,M	FS,PS	N
Mahonia repens	Creeping Mahonia	L,M	FS,PS,SH	N
Pinus edulis	Piñon Pine	L,M	FS	N
Shepherdia rotundifolia	Roundleaf Buffaloberry	L,M	FS	N
Yucca baccata	Datil	L,M	FS	N
Yucca elata	Soap Tree Yucca	L,M	FS	N
Yucca glauca	Rocky Mountain Yucca	L,M	FS	N
Yucca harrimaniae	Harriman's Yucca	L,M	FS	N

ORNAMENTAL GRASSES

Botanic Name	Familiar Name	Water Zone	Light	Native Origin
Agropyron cristatum	Crested Wheatgrass	M±	FS	N
Andropogon gerardii	Big Bluestem	M±	FS	N
❀ *Andropogon scoparius*	Little Bluestem	M±	FS	N
❀ *Bouteloua curtipendula*	Sideoats Grama	L,M	FS	N
Bouteloua gracilis	Blue Grama	L,M	FS	N
❀ *Koeleria cristata* (syn. *Koeleria pyramidata*)	Junegrass	M±	FS	N
Oryzopsis hymenoides	Indian Ricegrass	L,M	FS	N
❀ *Sorghastrum nutans*	Indiangrass	M±	FS	N
Stipa comata	Needle-and-thread Grass	M±	FS	N

TELLING TEMPERATURE BY COUNTING CRICKET CHIRPS

By counting cricket chirps, it is possible to tell the temperature (near the cricket) plus or minus 1°F. There are two methods to do this.

1. Count the chirps in one minute.
2. Divide by 5.
3. Add 43.
4. This equals the Fahrenheit temperature ± 1°.

   or

1. Count the chirps in 14 seconds.
2. Add 40.
3. This equals the Fahrenheit temperature ± 1°. ∎

Plants with Great Waterwise Potential

These plants are included to give enthusiastic gardeners and ambitious nurseries more plants to consider for various watering zones. Because the watering zones indicated are based on limited observations, however, an experimental approach is suggested.

The amounts of water indicated (in inches per week) refer to Denver midsummer irrigation needs, during periods without rain. The figures (in gallons of water per square foot) refer to irrigation needed for a typical 20-week irrigation season.

High Watering Zones:	Moderate Watering Zones:	Low Watering Zones:
■ 18-20 gals. added per sq. ft. per 20-week season	■ 10± gals. added per sq. ft. per 20-week season	■ 0 to 3 gals. added per sq. ft. per 20-week season
■ .5″ added 3 times per week	■ .75″ added once per week	■ .5″ added every other week
■ Approx. 30″ added over 20 wks.	■ Approx. 16″ added over 20 wks.	■ Approx. 4.5″ added over 20 wks.
Typical plants: Kentucky Bluegrass lawns, Redtwig Dogwood, Pansies	*Typical plants: Turf-type Tall Fescue lawns, Potentilla, Purple Coneflower*	*Typical plants: Buffalograss lawns, Rabbitbrush, Mexican Hat Coneflower*

KEY TO PLANT LIST SYMBOLS

❀ = Plants with detailed descriptions
H = High watering zone
M = Moderate watering zone
L = Low watering zone
N = Native to the Rocky Mountain region
FS = Full sun
PS = Part sun
SH = Shade
± = An ability to survive in conditions somewhat more or less than a single category

HERBACEOUS FLOWERS

Botanic Name	Familiar Name	Water Zone	Light	Native Origin
Acantholimon spp.	Prickly Thrift species	L,M?	FS	Eurasia
Acantholimon hohenakeri	Spikethrift	L,M?	FS	Eurasia
Agastache barberi	—	M±?	FS	S.west U.S.
Agastache pallidiflora	Yellow Mint	M±?	FS	C. Ariz., N.M., Rocky Mtns.
Allium caeruleum	—	L,M?	FS	Central Asia
Allium giganteum	—	L,M?	FS	Central Asia
Allium karataviense	—	L,M?	FS	Central Asia
Allium oreophilum	—	L,M?	FS	Central Asia
Alyssoides utriculata	—	L,M	FS	Mtns. of c. Eur.
Alyssum montanum	—	M±?	FS	Medit. region
Amsonia arenaria	Arenaria Blue Star	L,M?	FS	W. Tex., Ariz., Mex.
Amsonia ciliata	Fringed Blue Star	L,M?	FS,PS	C. Tex.
Amsonia jonesii	Jones' Blue Star	L,M?	FS	Ut., Ariz., W. Colo.
Amsonia longiflora	Tubular Slimpod	L,M?	FS	S. New Mex., W. Tex.
Amsonia tomentosa	Feltleaf Blue Star	L,M?	FS	S.w. N. Amer.
Anacyclus depressus	Atlas Daisy	L,M?	FS	Morocco
Anaphalis cinnamomea	Pearly Everlasting	L,M?	FS,PS	India
Anaphalis margaritacea	Pearly Everlasting	L,M?	FS,PS	N
Anchusa azurea 'Dropmore' (syn. *A. italica 'Dropmore'*)	Anchusa	M±?	FS	Medit. region
Anemone blanda	Windflower	L,M?	FS	Asia Minor–Turkestan
Anthemis biebersteiniana	Bieberstein Marguerite	M±?	FS	?
Anthemis tinctoria	Golden Marguerite	M±?	FS	Eurasia
Arabis spp.	Rockcress species	L,M?	FS,PS	N. Amer., Euras.
Armeria maritima	Common Thrift	L,M?	FS	Europe
Arum italicum 'Pictum'	Arum	M±?	SH	Medit. region
Aster alpinus	Alpine Aster	L,M?	FS	Eurasia
Aster novae-angliae	New England Aster	M±?	FS	N. Amer.
Aster novi-belgii	New York Aster	M±?	FS	N. Amer.
Aubrieta deltoidea	Rockcress	L,M?	FS,PS	Medit. region
Aubrieta olympica	Greek Rockcress	L,M?	FS,PS	Medit. region
Baptisia australis	Wild Indigo	L,M?	FS,PS	E. North Amer.
Barbarea vulgaris	Wintercress	M±?	FS	Europe
Belamcanda chinensis	Blackberry Lily	L,M?	FS,PS	China
Borago officinalis	Borage	M±?	FS,PS	Medit. region
Calceolaria lanceolata	—	M±?	FS	S. Amer.

Botanic Name	Familiar Name	Water Zone	Light	Native Origin
Campanula formanekiana	—	L,M?	FS,PS	Greece, Bulgaria
Campanula incurva	—	M±?	FS,PS	Greece
Campanula lyrata	—	L,M?	FS,PS	Greece, Albania
Centaurea bella	Rock Cornflower	L,M?	FS	Caucasus
Centaurea conifera (syn. *Leuzea conifera*)	—	M±?	FS	Spain, Algeria
Centaurea dealbata	Rose Cornflower	L,M?	FS	Caucasus
Centaurea macrocephala	Yellow Cornflower	L,M?	FS	Caucasus
Centaurea montana	Mountain Bluet	L,M?	FS	Eurasia
Centaurea rothrockii	—	M±?	FS	S.e. Ariz., S.w. New Mex., Rocky Mtns.
Cephalaria tatarica	—	L,M?	FS	Cauc., c. Asia
Ceratostigma plumbaginoides	Plumbago	L,M?	FS,PS	W. China
Chamaemelum nobile	Chamomile	M±?	FS,PS	Medit. region
Chamaespartium sagittale (syn. *Genista sagittalis*)	—	L,M?	FS	Eur. to W. Asia
Cheiranthus allionii (syn. *Erysimum hieraciifloium*)	Wallflower	M±?	FS,PS	Medit. to Himls.
Chrysanthemum haradjanii (syn. *Tanacetum densum amani*)	Partridge Feather	M?	FS	Syria
Chrysanthemum weyrichii	Weyrich Chrysanthemum	L,M?	FS	Japan
Clematis alpina	Alpine Clematis	M±?	FS,PS	Asia
Clematis integrifolia	—	M±?	FS,PS	Europe, Asia
Colchicum spp.	Colchicum species	M±?	FS	Europe, Asia
Coreopsis verticillata 'Moonbeam'	Moonbeam Coreopsis	L,M?	FS	Cultivar
Cotula potentillina	—	M±?	FS	New Zealand
Cyclamen coum	—	M±?	PS±	S.e. Europe
Cyclamen hederifolium	—	M±?	PS±	Greece to Iran
Delosperma ashtonii	—	L,M?	FS	Southern Africa
Delosperma sutherlandii	—	L,M?	FS	Southern Africa
Delphinium grandiflorum	—	L,M?	FS	China, Japan
Dianthus spp.	Pinks	L,M?	FS	
Dianthus × 'Allwoodii'	Allwood Pink	L,M?	FS	Cultivar
Dianthus freynii	Freynii Pink	L,M?	FS	Alpine Balkan
Dianthus nardiformis	Nardiformis Pink	L,M?	FS	Europe
Dianthus nitidus	Nitidus Pink	L,M?	FS	Europe
Dianthus plumarius var.	Cottage Pinks	L,M?	FS	Europe
Dianthus simulans	Simulens Pink	L,M?	FS	?
Dictamnus albus (syn. *Dictamnus grandiflora*)	Gas Plant	L,M?	FS,PS	S. Eur. to N. China
Digitalis ferruginea	—	L,M?	FS,PS	Greece
Digitalis grandiflora (syn. *ambigua*)	—	L,M?	FS,PS	S. Europe

Botanic Name	Familiar Name	Water Zone	Light	Native Origin
Digitalis lutea	Yellow Foxglove	L,M?	FS,PS	S. Eur. to n. Chi.
Dracocephalum spp.	Dragonhead species	L,M?	FS	Eurasia
Dracocephalum purdomii	—	L,M?	FS	N.w. China
Ecballium elaterium	Squirting Cucumber	L,M?	FS	Medit. region
Echinops ritro	Globe Thistle	L,M?	FS	E. Eur. to W. Asia
Eranthis cilicica	Eranthis	L,M?	FS,PS	Asia Minor to c. Asia
Eranthis hyemalis	Winter Aconite	L,M?	FS,PS	S. Europe
Eremurus spp.	Eremurus species	L,M?	FS	Central Asia
Erigeron spp.	Erigeron species	L,M?	FS,PS	N
Erigeron compositus	Fernleaf Fleabane	L,M?	FS,PS	N
Eriogonum spp.	Eriogonum species	L,M?	FS	N
Eriogonum corymbosum	Corym Buckwheat	L,M?	FS	Utah
Eriogonum effusum	Wild Buckwheat	L,M?	FS	N
Eriogonum ovalifolium	—	L,M?	FS	N
Eryngium spp.	Sea Holly species	L,M?	FS	Medit. to Cauc.
Euphorbia anacampseros	—	L,M?	FS	Medit. region
Euphorbia rigida	—	L,M?	FS	Medit. region
Euryops acraeus	Drakensberg Daisy	L,M?	FS	S. Africa
Filipendula vulgaris (syn. *Filipendula hexapetala*)	Filipendula, Dropwort	L,M?	FS	Eurasia
Fritillaria bucharica	Bucharica Fritillaria	L,M?	FS	Central Asia
Fritillaria eduardii	—	L,M?	FS	C. Asia, esp. Tadzhikistan
Fritillaria pallidiflora	—	M±?	FS	C. Asia to s. Siberia
Gaura lindheimeri	White Gaura	L,M	FS	Tex., La., Mex.
Gentiana affinis	Prairie Gentian	L,M?	FS	N
Geranium spp.	Hardy Geranium species and varieties	M±?	FS,PS	—
Geum triflorum	Prairie Smoke	L,M?	FS	N
Haplopappus acaulis	Stemless Goldenweed	L,M?	FS	N
Haplopappus glutinosus	Mat Daisy	L,M?	FS	Chile, Argen.
Haplopappus spinulosus	Cutleaf Goldenweed	L,M?	FS	N
Helianthemum apenninum	Silver Sunrose	L,M?	FS	S. Eur. to Asia M.
Helianthemum nummularium	Sunrose	L,M?	FS	S. Europe
Helichrysum bellum	—	L,M?	FS	S. Africa
Helichrysum tianschanicum	Curryplant	L,M?	FS	Central Asia
Helichrysum trilineatum	—	L,M?	FS	S. Africa
Helichrysum virgineum	—	L,M?	FS	Greece
Hieracium lanatum	Woolly Hawkweed	L,M?	FS	S. Europe

Botanic Name	Familiar Name	Water Zone	Light	Native Origin
Iberis sempervirens	Candytuft	L,M?	FS,PS	S. Europe
Incarvillea compacta	—	L,M?	PS,FS	Tibet
Incarvillea delavayi	—	L,M?	PS,FS	Eastern China
Incarvillea emodi	—	L,M?	PS,FS	Afghanistan
Incarvillea lutea	—	L,M?	PS,FS	W. and c. China
Incarvillea olgae	—	L,M?	PS,FS	Central Asia
Inula helenium	—	L,M?	FS	Central Asia
Inula magnifica	—	L,M?	FS	Caucasus
Ipomoea leptophylla	Bush Morning Glory	L,M?	FS	N
Iris graeberana	—	L,M?	FS	?
Iris iberica elegantissima	—	L,M?	FS	Turkey, Iran, Armenia
Iris spuria halophila	—	L,M?	FS	Asia
Iris warleyensis	—	L,M?	FS	C. Asia, esp. Tadzhikistan
Lilium pumilum	Coral Lily	L,M?	FS,PS	Mongolia, Gobi Desert
Linum flavum	Yellow Flax	L,M?	FS	C. and s. Eur.
Lupinus spp.	Lupines	L,M?	FS	N
Macleaya cordata	Plume Poppy	L,M?	FS,PS	China, Japan
Malva spp.	Mallows	L,M?	FS	—
Mertensia spp.	Mertensias	L,M?	FS	N
Michauxia tchihatchewii	Michauxia	L,M?	FS	Medit. region
Morina persica	Persian Whorlplant	L,M?	FS	Central Asia
Nepeta concolor	—	L,M?	FS	Turkey
Oenothera lavandulifolia (syn. *Calylophus lavandulifolius*)	—	L,M?	FS	N
Oenothera pallida	Pale Evening Primrose	L,M?	FS	Colo., Wyo., Ut.
Oenothera serrulata	Evening Primrose	L,M?	FS	Great Plains
Oenothera tetragona	Evening Primrose	L,M?	FS	N. Amer.
Papaver orientale	Oriental Poppy	L,M?	FS,PS	S.w. Asia
Phlomis russeliana	Jerusalem Sage	L,M?	FS	Asia Minor
Phlomis tuberosa	—	L,M?	FS	Eur. to c. Asia
Phlox mesoleuca var.	Mesoleuca phlox varieties	L,M?	FS	N. Mex., New Mex.
Physostegia virginiana	Obedience Plant	L,M?	FS	E. North Amer.
Platycodon grandiflorus	Balloon Flower	L,M?	FS,PS	E. Asia
Potentilla hippiana	Woolly Cinquefoil	L,M?	FS	N
Ptilotrichum macrocarpum	—	L,M?	FS	S. France
Ptilotrichum spinosum 'Roseum'	—	L,M?	FS	Mor., s. Spain

Botanic Name	Familiar Name	Water Zone	Light	Native Origin
Rosa spp.	Rose species	M±	FS	—
Rosa Hultheimia persica	—	M±?	FS	?
Ruta graveolens	Rue	L,M?	FS	S. Europe
Salvia argentea	Silver Salvia	L,M?	FS	S. Europe
Salvia baldschuanica	—	L,M?	FS,PS	Central Asia
Salvia bulleyana	—	L,M?	SH,PS	Himalayas
Salvia cadmica	—	L,M?	FS	Asia Minor
Salvia candidissima	—	L,M?	FS	?
Salvia cyanescens	—	L,M?	FS,PS?	Turkey
Salvia davidsonii	—	L,M?	FS,PS	S. Ariz.
Salvia forskaohlei	—	L,M?	SH	Turkey
Salvia frigida	—	L,M?	FS	Turkey
Salvia haematocalyx	—	L,M?	FS	S.e. Europe
Salvia hians	—	L,M?	SH	Kashmir
Salvia hypargeia	—	L,M?	FS	Turkey
Salvia lemmonii	—	L,M?	FS	S. Ariz.
Salvia limbata	—	L,M?	FS	Caucacus
Salvia lyrata	Cancer Weed	L,M?	SH	Eastern U.S.
Salvia microstegia	—	L,M?	FS	Turkey
Salvia pratensis	Meadow Clary	L,M?	FS	Eur., Morocco
Salvia ringens	—	L,M?	FS,PS?	Balkans
Salvia sclarea	Clary	L,M?	FS,PS	S. Eur. to c. Asia
Salvia × superba	—	L,M?	FS	Hybrid
Schivereckia podolica	—	L,M?	FS	Central Asia
Scilla spp.	Squill species	L,M?	FS,PS	Africa, Eur., Asia
Silphium laciniatum	Compass Plant	L,M?	FS	Great Plains
Stachys alopecuros	—	L,M?	FS	S. and c. Europe
Stachys germanica	—	L,M?	FS	Eur., n. Africa, C. Asia
Stachys inflata	—	L,M?	FS	Central Asia
Stanleya pinnata	Prince's Plume	L,M?	FS	N
Tanacetum parthenium (syn. *Chrysanthemum parthenium*)	Feverfew	M±?	FS,PS	S.e. Europe
Tanacetum vulgare	Tansy	M±?	FS,PS	Eur. and Asia
Teucrium chamaedrys	Wall Germander	L,M?	FS,PS	S.w. Eur. to Asia Minor
Thelesperma ambiguum	Showy Navajo Tea	L?	FS	N
Thelesperma filifolium	Greenthread	L?	FS	N
Thelesperma megapotamicum	Navajo Tea	L?	FS	N
Thermopsis fabacea	Fabacea Thermopsis	L,M?	FS	Kamchatka, Kurile Island
Tiarella cordifolia var. *collina* (syn. *Tiarella wherryi*)	Foamflower	M±?	SH,PS	S.east U.S.

Botanic Name	Familiar Name	Water Zone	Light	Native Origin
Tulipa aucherana	—	L,M?	FS	Central Asia
Tulipa humilis	—	L,M?	FS	Central Asia
Verbascum spp.	Verbascum species	L,M?	FS	Asia, Eur., N. Africa
Verbascum bombyciferum	—	L,M?	FS	Asia Minor
Verbascum densiflorum	—	L,M?	FS	Europe
Verbascum olympicum	Greek Verbascum	L,M?	FS	Greece
Verbascum phoeniceum	—	L,M?	FS	Asia Minor
Verbascum thapsus	Flannel Plant	L,M?	FS	Eurasia
Verbascum undulatum	—	L,M?	FS	S. Medit.
Verbascum wiedemannianum	—	L,M?	FS	Asia Minor
Verbena canadensis	Rose Verbena	L,M?	FS	N
Verbena tenera	Maonetti Pink Verbena	L,M?	FS	S. Brazil
Verbena tenuisecta	Purple Moss Verbena	L,M?	FS	S. America
Veronica spp.	Veronica species	M±	FS,PS	N. Hemisphere
Veronica kotschyana	—	M±	FS,PS	Turkey
Veronica liwanensis	Turkish Veronica	M±	PS±	Asia Minor
Veronica pectinata	Woolly Veronica	M±	PS±	Asia Minor
Waldsteinia ternata	—	L,M?	FS,PS	C. Eur. to Japan

SHRUBS

Botanic Name	Familiar Name	Water Zone	Light	Native Origin
Acaena myriophylla	—	M±?	FS,PS,SH	Chile
Cercocarpus brevifolius	Hairy Mountain Mahogany	L,M?	FS	N
Chamaespartium sagittale (syn. *Genista sagittalis*)	Winged Broom	M±?	FS	Spain, Port.
Cytisus spp.	Broom species	L,M?	FS	Medit. region
Cytisus nigricans	—	M±?	FS	Spain, Port.
Cytisus × praecox	Warminster Broom	M±?	FS	Spain, Port.
Cytisus ratisbonensis	—	M±?	FS	Spain, Port.
Cytisus scoparius	Scotch Broom	M±?	FS	Spain, Port.
Dalea formosa	Feather Dalea	L,M?	FS	N
Ephedra americana var. *andina*	—	L,M?	FS	S. America
Ephedra equisetina	—	L,M?	FS	Asia
Ephedra erinacea pungens	Lavender Broom	M±?	FS	Spain, Mor.
Ephedra gerardiana	—	L,M?	FS	Asia
Ephedra minima	—	L,M?	FS	Tibet, China
Ephedra minuta	—	L,M?	FS	Tibet
Ephedra regeliana	—	L,M?	FS	Asia
Fraxinus anomala	Singleleaf Ash	L,M?	FS	N
Genista spp.	Broom species	L,M?	FS	Eur., n. Africa, W. Asia
Peraphyllum ramosissimum	Squawapple	L,M?	FS	N
Prunus andersonii	Desert Peach	L,M?	FS	N
Prunus fasciculata	Desert Almond	L,M	FS	Calif., Ut., Ariz.
Ptelea trifoliata	Hoptree	L,M?	FS	N

Explanation of the Plant Profiles

Type of Plant This information is included to serve as a quick guide, especially in selecting lower-maintenance or higher-maintenance herbaceous flowers.

Flowers The flowering times indicated here represent the usual blooming time in Boulder, Colorado. Plants that tend to prefer hot conditions often bloom several weeks earlier at the Denver Botanic Gardens.

Other Features This is included to indicate when the flowers are just one significant ornamental feature of a plant that is described.

Height and Spread This is extremely variable with most plants, and the figures included here indicate typical rather than maximum dimensions.

Culture This information is meant as a quick guide to soil, sun/shade preference, water requirements, and other cultural preferences. Many of these plants are likely to perform well under much wider conditions, if not all of the cultural aspects are taken to extremes, and if some variation in performance is acceptable.

Wildlife Deer browsing (and lack of browsing), as well as butterfly and hummingbird activity are the main observations included. These observations are based on first-hand experience primarily by gardeners in Boulder, Colorado, with specific information from other areas included when available. Unfortunately, little information about rabbit nibbling was available.

Natural Range This is included both because it is interesting and because it gives some idea about probable cultural conditions that may be important. Many sources were used, but it is impossible to be totally inclusive, because new observations are frequently expanding the known ranges of most of these plants.

Landscape Uses This is meant to provide a few quick ideas about using these wonderful plants.

Propagation Many of these plants are so new to artificial propagation that it is literally impossible to be definitive at this time. The bibliography gives additional sources of information about propagation of many of these plants. The primary purpose of including information about propagation is to help expand use of these plants by offering at least one idea about propagation of each plant described.

Notes The fascinating facts and tantalizing tidbits about many of these plants seem endless. The purpose of the small amount of information included here is to help foster an interest and an appreciation for the native flora of this region, as well as for appropriately introduced flora.

HERBACEOUS FLOWERS

ACHILLEA LANULOSA
(syn. Achillea millefolium var. lanulosa)

Native White Yarrow

Type of Plant	Long-lived perennial.
Flowers	White. Flat clusters. May to September, depending on weather.
Other Features	Medium green, somewhat lacy or fern-like foliage.
Height	1 to 2 feet. **Spread** Variable. Invasiveness is possible, but rare in dry situations.
Culture	*Moderate watering zones,* but will grow well with somewhat more or less water. Full sun to part shade. Does best in moderate to low fertility soil with good drainage.
Wildlife	Rarely browsed by deer if grown somewhat dry.
Natural Range	Much of North America including Canada, the United States, and Mexico.
Landscape Use	Attractive singly in gardens or scattered in meadows.
Propagation	Seed (no stratification needed), and division.
Notes	Since ancient times, yarrows have been associated with healing, especially with the stopping of bleeding. The name *Achillea* is a reference to Achilles, who is reputed to have discovered some of these healing properties. It is said that Native Americans chewed the leaves to numb the mouth as a treatment for toothaches, and some Indian groups considered oil extracted from yarrow as a soothing treatment for burns, as well as a contraceptive and an abortive. *Achillea* × *'Coronation Gold'* is a tall (2 to 3 feet), yellow, hybrid variety. *Achillea* × *'Moonshine'* is a medium height (1 to 2 feet) hybrid variety with silver foliage. Neither of these varieties has spreading tendencies, and both appear to be considerably more drought-tolerant than *Achillea millefolium* varieties. There are numerous other varieties and species; some are very low-growing and useful as ground covers for limited areas.

AGASTACHE CANA

Double Bubble Mint

Type of Plant	Long-lived perennial.
Flowers	Pink. Has fragrance like Double Bubble bubblegum. Late July to mid-October.
Other Features	Foliage is fragrant, but different from the flower fragrance.
Height	To 3 feet. **Spread** To 2 feet.
Culture	*Moderate watering zones,* but will do well with either somewhat more or less water. Full sun. Grows well in a wide range of soils, but overwatering is likely to be a problem in clay.
Wildlife	Very good for attracting hummingbirds and hawkmoths over a long period of time.
Natural Range	New Mexico and west Texas.
Landscape Use	A very showy, easily grown, long-lived perennial, for sunny, semiarid flower gardening. Potentially a very good plant for wildflower meadows, but limited availability of seed is likely to be a problem.
Propagation	Easily grown from seed, stratified for two months.
Notes	This plant is considered rare and endangered in New Mexico, where it is known on only five sites in four counties. These sites are in mountainous locations between about five and six thousand feet.

BERLANDIERA LYRATA

Chocolate Flower

Type of Plant	Long-lived perennial.
Flowers	Yellow, daisy-like, with a fragrance like warm milk chocolate. Early June through fall. In hot weather, flowers fade by midmorning and reopen the next day. Deadheading is not needed to maintain continuous blooming.
Height	1 foot or more. **Spread** 2 feet or more.
Culture	*Low watering zones.* Continuously wet conditions, especially during the winter, will cause problems. Good drainage is important. Denver appears to be near the northern limit of reliable hardiness. Farther north, or at higher altitudes, success is likely to depend on warm microclimates. Highly fertile soil is not desirable. Clay is satisfactory if not overwatered. Full sun.
Wildlife	Deer appear to avoid this plant totally.
Natural Range	Extreme southeastern Colorado and southwestern Kansas southward.
Landscape Use	A delightful, showy "conversation piece." Use singly or in masses in flower gardens. A good candidate for midgrass and shortgrass meadows.
Propagation	Easily grown from seed. Stratification not needed. Under favorable conditions a few flowers can be expected the first year. Some seedlings can be expected, but only small plants will transplant successfully, because of a deep root system.
Notes	Unusual in commercial nurseries, but seed is available from several regional seed companies. Seed is easily collected from garden plants.

CALLIRHOE INVOLUCRATA

Poppy Mallow

Type of Plant	Long-lived perennial.
Flowers	Reddish-purple. June to October.
Height	6 to 8 inches. **Spread** 2 feet or more.
Culture	*Low watering zones.* Moderate watering is acceptable if the soil is well drained. Full sun. Roots are carrotlike, making transplanting very difficult. Only very small plants can be transplanted without serious setback. Some seedlings are often reported. With too much water, plants tend to become somewhat bare in the center.
Wildlife	Deer have avoided this plant in some gardens.
Natural Range	Great Plains from Canada to Mexico and westward to Utah.
Landscape Use	Good for filling in around other taller plants, because of the low, spreading form. The reddish-purple color is extremely striking with the soft blue of Russian Sage (*Perovskia atriplicifolia*).
Propagation	Usually by seed. No stratification is needed, but patience is in order since seeds will sometimes continue to germinate (a few at a time) for a year or more.
Notes	The Lakota Indian name, *ezhuta nantiazilia*, refers to medicinal smoke. Roots have been reported to taste somewhat like sweet potatoes. The leaves are said to have a pleasant taste, and are said to be useful (like okra) in thickening soup.

CENTRANTHUS RUBER

Jupiter's Beard, Red Valerian

Type of Plant	Short-lived perennial.
Flowers	Light pink to reddish pink. Late June into September.
Other Features	Attractive, succulent, blue-green leaves.
Height	Usually to 3 feet. **Spread** To 2½ feet.
Culture	*Moderate and low watering zones.* Once established, this plant is very enduring in most circumstances. In very moist, very fertile soil, however, there might be some problems. Numerous seedlings are frequently reported, but it is usually not considered invasive. Deadheading will nearly eliminate this problem.
Wildlife	Butterflies are reported to visit this plant frequently.
Natural Range	Mediterranean region. Naturalized in parts of the western United States.
Landscape Use	A very showy plant for low and moderate watering zones, blooming over a very long season.
Propagation	Usually by seed. Seedlings display considerable variation in flower color, with occasional white-flowered plants.
Notes	Setwall is one of the old names for this plant, and refers to the proliferation of Jupiter's Beard in old stone walls in northern Europe.

COREOPSIS LANCEOLATA

Lanceleaf Coreopsis

Type of Plant	Long-lived perennial (usually more than three years).
Flowers	Bright yellow, daisy-like. June through September.
Height	Usually about 1 to 2 feet. **Spread** 1 to 2 feet.
Culture	*Moderate watering zones*. Somewhat more or less water is also acceptable. Well-drained soil, with not more than moderate fertility, is especially important if more than moderate water is likely. Full sun is best. Deadheading will keep the plant blooming. Abundant seedlings are common.
Wildlife	No reports available.
Natural Range	Eastern United States.
Landscape Use	Attractive singly or in groups. Potentially a showy addition to midgrass and tallgrass meadows.
Propagation	Division is the most reliable way to assure desired characteristics of specific varieties.
Notes	*Coreopsis lanceolata* is reported to be more drought tolerant than *C. grandiflora*, which is very similar in appearance. "Tickseed," one of the names for this plant, comes from a description of the seed.

DELOSPERMA COOPERI

Hardy Pink Ice Plant

Type of Plant	Long-lived ground cover.
Flowers	Shocking pink. Late spring (May) to late fall (October).
Other Features	Attractive, succulent evergreen foliage.
Height	Usually under 6 inches. **Spread** Variable to about 2 feet.
Culture	*Low watering zones.* Dry, lean soil. Full sun. Deadheading not needed.
Wildlife	Seldom browsed by deer.
Natural Range	Southern Africa.
Landscape Use	An excellent groundcover by itself, or an excellent plant to fill in around other plants.
Propagation	Seed or cuttings.
Notes	*Delosperma nubigenum* (*congestum?*), Hardy Yellow Ice Plant, is similar, except the yellow flowers occur all at once in early summer, and the foliage turns a reddish color in the fall. This plant was introduced in 1980 at the Denver Botanic Gardens by Panayoti Kelaidis, acting on a suggestion by Robert Putnam, a great plant enthusiast from Washington state. There is uncertainty, at present, about the correct species name. Currently, however, it is best known by the species name *nubigenum*.

DIGITALIS LANATA

Grecian Foxglove

Type of Plant	Short-lived perennial.
Flowers	Cream-colored flowers on long spikes. Late June into September.
Height	Variable, to 4 feet. **Spread** 1 to 2 feet.
Culture	*Moderate to low watering zones.* Full sun to light shade. Well-adapted to a wide range of soils, but will not tolerate soggy soil. Deadheading occasionally will encourage continued blooming. Leave some seed for production of seedlings to replace older plants.
Wildlife	Deer have not been reported to browse this plant.
Natural Range	Eastern Mediterranean region.
Landscape Use	A striking plant for dry or moderate watering zones in waterwise gardens.
Propagation	Seed. Flowering usually occurs the second year.
Notes	"*Digitalis*," the genus name, is derived from the Latin word for finger, or more likely, finger of a glove. The reference to "fox" in the English language name "Foxglove" is probably an alteration of "folk," as in "Folk's glove." *Digitalis grandiflora* (syn. *Digitalis ambiguua*; Giant Yellow Foxglove) has been a vigorous, long-lived perennial for full sun and light shade and moderate to low watering zones at the Denver Botanic Gardens. It was introduced by Jim and Jenny Archibald. *Digitalis ferruginea* (Rusty Foxglove) is another foxglove for use in similar areas.

ECHINACEA PURPUREA

Purple Coneflower

Type of Plant	Long-lived perennial.
Flowers	Purple with decorative centers. July and August.
Other Features	Seed heads are very showy, and last well into winter.
Height	About 3 feet. **Spread** About 2 feet.
Culture	*Moderate watering zones.* If too dry, this plant will be much smaller, and it will die out completely in very dry conditions. Full sun is best. Most soils are acceptable. Abundant seedlings are common.
Wildlife	Rarely browsed by deer. Frequently attracts numerous butterflies.
Natural Range	Central United States, in moist grasslands.
Landscape Use	Attractive singly or in groups. An attractive addition to midgrass and tallgrass meadows, where moisture is adequate.
Propagation	Seed. Stratification not needed.
Notes	"*Echinacea*" is Greek for hedgehog, an interesting reference to the bristly flower centers. Several species of the genus are frequently mentioned in herbal literature for numerous medicinal remedies. Native Americans of the plains used this plant to soothe insect and snakebites. Pieces of roots were chewed to relieve toothaches. Recent immunological studies suggest that extracts of this plant increase interferon production, and therefore partially verify belief that this plant helps fight influenza and herpes viruses.

EUSTOMA GRANDIFLORUM
Tulip Gentian

Type of Plant	Short-lived perennial.
Flowers	Usually dark blue, sometimes white or pink. Late July into September.
Height	1 to 2 feet. **Spread** 8 to 12 inches.
Culture	*Moderate to high watering zones.* Full sun and part shade. Plants often recover well from extremely dry conditions, but they don't grow well in dry conditions.
Wildlife	No reports available.
Natural Range	Formerly South Dakota into Mexico, in moist grasslands.
Landscape Use	Showiest in groups, in moist areas of gardens. This plant would tend to be hidden by mid and tall grasses and needs more water than shortgrass meadows.
Propagation	Seed is extremely small (like dust). Stratification is probably not needed. Sowing seed in January (indoors) will usually produce summer bloom. Blooming appears to be triggered by day length.
Notes	Agriculture, gravel mining, and urbanization have destroyed most natural populations in Colorado and many other areas. *Eustoma grandiflorum* is now considered rare and endangered in Colorado. The florist trade knows this plant as *Lisianthus russellianus*.

GILIA AGGREGATA (syn. Ipomopsis aggregata)
Scarlet Gilia

Type of Plant	Biennial.
Flowers	Bright red spikes, occasionally pink. July and August, occasionally earlier and later.
Other Features	An attractive rosette the first year.
Height	To 3 feet. **Spread** To 1 foot or more.
Culture	*Low watering zones.* Well-drained soil. Full sun. Some seedlings can be expected to help replace plants that will die after blooming.
Wildlife	Very good for attracting hummingbirds, but deer aggressively browse plants that are unprotected with repellents or fences.
Natural Range	California to British Columbia, east to the Rocky Mountains.
Landscape Use	Attractive singly or in groups in gardens or meadows.
Propagation	Somewhat erratic, but not difficult from seed. Stratification not needed.
Notes	One study concluded that *Gilia aggregata* plants in the Flagstaff, Arizona, area change from red to light pink to attract hummingbird pollination early in the season, and then hawkmoth pollination after the hummingbirds migrate north. In Nederland, Colorado, however, all of the Gilia plants are light pink all season, and hummingbirds are resident pollinators throughout the summer.

GUTIERREZIA SAROTHRAE

Snakeweed

Type of Plant	Long-lived perennial.
Flowers	Bright yellow, totally covering the plant. September to October.
Other Features	Foliage is attractive, but is not of major ornamental value.
Height	12 to 18 inches. **Spread** 12 to 18 inches.
Culture	*Low watering zones.* Well-drained soil. Full sun.
Wildlife	Deer do not browse snakeweed.
Natural Range	Manitoba to northern Mexico, westward to Washington and California.
Landscape Use	A very showy, late-blooming perennial. Attractive when used singly in gardens or scattered in shortgrass meadows. In a few areas, this plant is considered aggressive enough to raise questions about the wisdom of its use. This has not been the experience in other areas, however, and deadheading the plant will completely control this. Case-by-case judgment seems the best policy.
Propagation	Seed. Stratification not needed.
Notes	Because cattle won't eat snakeweed, it multiplies rapidly on overgrazed rangeland. Native Americans made a tea from the leaves and roots to treat malaria, snakebites, and rheumatism. It is reported to be so effective in treating painful joints that it could be considered as a replacement or an alternative for aspirin. It was used by the Navajo for an attractive brownish-yellow dye.

HELIANTHUS MAXIMILIANI

Maximilian's Sunflower

Type of Plant	Long-lived perennial.
Flowers	Numerous small, yellow flowers arranged along the stem like hollyhock flowers. Late September to early October.
Other Features	Seeds are reported to be good wildlife food.
Height	5 to 10 feet. **Spread** To 3 feet.
Culture	*Moderate watering zones.* Will tolerate somewhat more or less water. Cut back stalks in early winter. Full sun.
Wildlife	Attracts numerous butterflies and bees.
Natural Range	Maine to North Carolina, west to Rocky Mountains, Canada to Texas.
Landscape Use	An attractive, very tall plant for late season color. Effective singly in large gardens, or scattered in midgrass and tallgrass meadows. "Hedges" of this sunflower make a showy fall display in northern New Mexico.
Propagation	Seed. No stratification needed. Also, root divisions.
Notes	On dry sites, this plant is quite small, sometimes only three feet high. Named for Prince Maximilian von Wied-Neu Wied who discovered the plant. The U.S. Department of Agriculture Soil Conservation Service Plant Materials Center in Knox City, Texas, has tested and released a variety called 'Aztec' Maximilian's Sunflower for range seeding in Texas and Oklahoma. Its seeds are eaten by various songbirds and quail. 'Prairie Gold' is another variety of Maximilian's Sunflower released by the Soil Conservation Service.

LIATRIS PUNCTATA

Dotted Gayfeather

Type of Plant	Long-lived perennial.
Flowers	Pink. August to September. Individual plants bloom for only about two weeks.
Height	1 to 1½ feet. **Spread** 1 to 1½ feet.
Culture	*Low watering zones.* Most soils, but good drainage and reduced moisture are important in clay. Full sun. Corms and tuberous taproots, possibly to fifteen foot depths, account for drought-enduring abilities.
Wildlife	Deer rarely browse this plant.
Natural Range	Great Plains grasslands from Canada to Mexico.
Landscape Use	A showy plant for dry gardens or shortgrass and midgrass meadows.
Propagation	Usually by seed. Takes more than one year to develop sufficiently to bloom. Germination is high with 1- to 2-month stratification. For meadow mixes, 3 seeds/square foot, or 10 lbs/acre have been recommended.
Notes	The large taproot is reported to be edible, but with extremely variable palatability. Liatris blooming begins with flowers at the top of the flower spike. This is quite unusual. *Liatris spicata* (common in the nursery trade) is *not* a low watering zone plant in this region. Collecting seed early in the season, from the top of the flower spike, may improve chances for obtaining viable seed.

LINUM PERENNE VAR. LEWISII

Lewis' Flax

Type of Plant	Short-lived perennial.
Flowers	Light blue. Open morning only, unless weather is cool and overcast. May through August.
Height	1 to 2 feet. **Spread** About 1 foot.
Culture	*Moderate watering zones.* Flax will also do well with somewhat more or less water. Well-drained soil. Preference for sandy soil. Full sun. Trimming off seeds in mid-summer often stimulates renewed blooming. Numerous seedlings are common and offer replacements for older plants that often die in their third or fourth year.
Wildlife	Deer browsing is moderate.
Natural Range	Western Great Plains from Canada to Mexico.
Landscape Use	Attractive singly or in groups in gardens. Also very attractive in shortgrass, midgrass, or tallgrass meadows.
Propagation	Usually by seed. Stratification not necessary.
Notes	This plant is closely related to the Eurasian Flax cultivated throughout history for linen fiber, linseed oil, and medicinal uses. *Linum perenne* var. *lewisii* is named for Meriwether Lewis of the Lewis and Clark Expedition. Native Americans used the tough fibrous stems to make twine, and there are also reports they used the seeds to flavor cooking.

MELAMPODIUM LEUCANTHUM
Blackfoot Daisy

Type of Plant	Short-lived perennial. In some situations, plants are considered long-lived.
Flowers	Numerous small, white daisy-like flowers. Continuous bloom from May into October.
Other Features	Flowers are reported to be fragrant in some situations.
Height	½ to 1 foot. **Spread** ½ to 1½ feet.
Culture	*Low watering zones.* Dry, gravelly soil preferred, but plants will grow well in clay if not overwatered. Full sun. Thrives in very hot situations. Higher and farther north than Denver, warm and dry microclimates are probably important for success. However, some seedlings can be expected even in areas beyond Denver. Seedlings offer a source of replacements for short-lived plants.
Wildlife	Deer haven't browsed these plants significantly.
Natural Range	Great Plains from southeastern Colorado and southwestern Kansas southward.
Landscape Use	A very showy, low-growing "filler" for dry gardens. Attractive singly or in masses. A beautiful addition to shortgrass meadows.
Propagation	Usually by seed. Stratification not needed. Seed is often considered difficult to germinate, but fresh seed germinates well in warm (70° to 75°F) soil. Giberellic acid treatment of seeds may improve germination. Propagation is also done from cuttings.
Notes	Blackfoot Daisy epitomizes the term "designer weed." Often associated with barren landscapes, this plant has great potential for warm, dry locations throughout much of the region.

MIRABILIS MULTIFLORA
Wild Four O'Clock

Type of Plant	Long-lived perennial. It may even outlive the gardener who plants it.
Flowers	Magenta trumpets. July to September, sometimes earlier and later. Flowers open in late afternoon and close during the morning, unless weather is cool and cloudy.
Height	Variable to 1½ feet. **Spread** Variable to 3 or 4 feet square.
Culture	*Low watering zones.* Well-drained soil is important. Clay soil may be best. Full sun or light, part shade. Dry conditions may be needed to initiate blooming. Root systems are extensive. Tops die back in early fall, and are easy to clean up when they break away at soil level.
Wildlife	Deer only occasionally browse Wild Four O'Clocks.
Natural Range	Southern Colorado and Utah to Mexico.
Landscape Use	The vigor of this plant can quickly overtake smaller neighboring plants. Effective in masses planted with Piñon Pines and native junipers.
Propagation	Germination not difficult (though only 50 percent is common) after one month stratification. Propagation by root cuttings is also possible.
Notes	This plant has a peculiar habit of disappearing (or skipping a year) now and then, but it has also been described as an immortal plant, apparently surviving occasional rototilling!

MONARDA FISTULOSA

Wild Monarda

Type of Plant	Long-lived perennial.
Flowers	Clusters of lavender flowers. Rarely white. July.
Other Features	Very fragrant foliage.
Height	About 2 feet. **Spread** Variable to about 2 feet.
Culture	*Moderate watering zones.* Most soils. Full sun to part shade. Plants often die back late in the season. Cutting back causes no harm and improves garden appearance.
Wildlife	Attracts many bees.
Natural Range	Scattered throughout the Great Plains.
Landscape Use	Attractive as single plants in gardens, or naturalized throughout midgrass and tallgrass meadows.
Propagation	Seed or division. Stratification not necessary, but seems to improve germination.
Notes	Monarda attempts to prevent self-pollination by shedding pollen from the anthers a day or two before the stigmas are receptive to the pollen. If there is insufficient bee pollination, plants will self-pollinate by curling their stigmas up into pollen exposed in the anthers. The British Earl Grey tea gets much of its distinctive flavor from Monarda. The species was named for the sixteenth-century medical botanist Nicholas de Monardes.

OENOTHERA CAESPITOSA

White-tufted Evening Primrose

Type of Plant	Perennial, usually short-lived.
Flowers	The large, white flowers open late in the day and close early the following day. They are delightfully fragrant. June through September.
Height	6 to 12 inches. **Spread** 12 to 18 inches.
Culture	*Low watering zones.* Well-drained soil is important. Full sun.
Wildlife	Hawkmoths are especially fond of this species. In some areas the seeds attract local birds.
Natural Range	Washington to California eastward to Colorado and New Mexico.
Landscape Use	Especially useful where the attractive flowers can be seen at close range, and where the fragrance can be appreciated.
Propagation	Usually by seed. Germination is somewhat erratic and slow. Stratification is probably helpful. Cool conditions favor germination.
Notes	The petals of all *Oenothera* species are connected directly to a slender floral tube which contains considerable amounts of nectar. These tubes are up to four inches long in *Oenothera caespitosa.* This apparently allows only long-tongued hawkmoths to extract the nectar. Since each flower may contain up to five or six drops of nectar (supplying about forty-two calories), and since the moths consume approximately eleven calories per minute while hovering, the value of this species to the moths is readily apparent. *Oenothera missouriensis* is yellow flowered and is one of many other species with considerable waterwise potential.

PENSTEMON BARBATUS

Scarlet Bugler

Type of Plant	Short-lived perennial.
Flowers	Bright red, on tall spikes. June to July.
Height	3 to 5 feet. **Spread** 1 to 1½ feet.
Culture	*Low watering zones.* Well-drained soil. Plants will adapt to clay, but overwatering is a likely problem. Plants live longer if grown dry. Full sun. Deadheading promotes a second bloom. Some seedlings can be expected and will help replace short-lived older plants.
Wildlife	Hummingbirds are regular visitors to this Penstemon. There are reports of black and yellow bumble bees tearing into the base of *Penstemon pinifolius* flowers to rob nectar without pollinating the flowers.
Natural Range	Colorado and Utah south into Mexico.
Landscape Use	Very striking used as single plants or in large groups. Groups of mixed species of Penstemons are also quite attractive.
Propagation	Most Penstemons need stratification for one to two months, then germinate easily. A few, such as *P. kunthii*, are easily grown from cuttings.
Notes	Pollination by hummingbirds is promoted by the red color, which is easily identified by the birds, but not by insects. Insects apparently see blue much better. The tubular shape of the flowers discourages bees, which must perch while extracting nectar.

OTHER PENSTEMONS:

P. alpinus (Alpine Penstemon) is similar to Rocky Mountain Penstemon but lighter blue and slightly later blooming.

P. barbatus 'Schooley's Yellow' is a striking yellow variety with numerous flower stems. It is named for Gussie Schooley, who found the first yellow variety of *P. barbatus*.

P. cobaea (Cobaea Penstemon). Very showy, large individual white flowers in a cluster. Maybe longer-lived than many penstemons and may spread slightly.

P. digitalis 'Husker Red' (Husker Red Penstemon). White clusters of flowers. Foliage is dark red when grown in sun. This penstemon will also grow in light shade.

P. kunthii is bright red. Flowers July to August. Another favorite of hummingbirds. It begins to bloom as *P. murrayanus* is finishing.

P. murrayanus (Murray's Penstemon) is dark red. Flowers June to July. A hummingbird favorite that begins to bloom as *P. barbatus* finishes.

P. pinifolius (Pineleaf Penstemon) is bright red. June flowers, tapering off through the summer. Low-growing with attractive, evergreen foliage.

P. pseudospectabilis (Showy Penstemon). Dazzling pink flowers on very tall spikes in June. Stems grow through the large blue-green leaves, creating an interesting effect that lasts into winter.

P. strictus (Rocky Mountain Penstemon) has dark blue flowers in June. Develops as a spreading clump and is longer-lived than most penstemons.

There are many additional, very attractive penstemons. *Hortus Third* has helpful descriptions of many of these.

PEROVSKIA ATRIPLICIFOLIA

Russian Sage

Type of Plant	Long-lived perennial.
Flowers	Large, light blue panicles.
Other Features	Fragrant foliage. Bracts add color long after flowers have faded.
Height	3 to 4 feet. **Spread** 3 to 4 feet.
Culture	*Moderate watering zones.* With more water, plants are likely to require staking. With less water, plants are likely to be much smaller. Most soils are satisfactory, but good drainage is important. Plants freeze back during the winter, but recover well in spring. Late spring freezes will kill developing foliage, but recovery is rapid. Plants sometimes spread moderately. Cutting back tops in late fall improves general appearance. Full sun.
Wildlife	Bees are attracted in great numbers. In some places, mantises can frequently be found stalking prey in the dissected foliage. In areas with very large deer herds, no browsing of this plant has ever been reported.
Natural Range	Eastern Iran, Afghanistan, Pakistan, Tibet.
Landscape Use	A striking plant for use in flower gardens, or among shrubs. The city of Arvada, Colorado, has used this plant successfully in large groups in arterial median plantings. Russian Sage planted with Pink Ice Plant (*Delosperma cooperi*), or Poppy Mallow (*Callirhoe involucrata*) creates a striking, "electric" color combination that lasts for many weeks.
Propagation	Seed, and by offshoots.
Notes	The genus is named for Vasili A. Perovski, a Russian governor of the former Orenberg province.

PSILOSTROPHE TAGETINA

Paperflower

Type of Plant	Short-lived perennial.
Flowers	Masses of small yellow flowers. June through September.
Other Features	Flowers gradually phase into a dry, tan-colored, papery condition, which is also quite ornamental.
Height	Usually to 2 feet. **Spread** Usually to 2 feet.
Culture	*Low watering zones.* Well-drained soil is important. Full sun. Paperflower thrives in hot situations. The plant will die within hours in wet rich soil, but thrives in soil that looks like dusty sand. Numerous seedlings can be expected, and serve well to replace short-lived older plants.
Wildlife	Paperflower has never been browsed in several neighborhoods with large deer herds.
Natural Range	Open sandy areas in New Mexico, Texas, Arizona, and northern Mexico.
Landscape Use	Very showy for a long period. Attractive used singly or in masses in gardens. Also attractive in short-grass meadows.
Propagation	Seeds. Stratification for about one month produces good germination in warm soil.
Notes	*Psilostrophe bakeri* is more compact, but is otherwise quite similar.

RATIBIDA COLUMNIFERA

Mexican Hat Coneflower

Type of Plant	Short-lived perennial. Most plants live about two to four years.
Flowers	Bright yellow, mahogany-red, or a combination. June to September. Some plants bloom through the entire season, others bloom for only part of the season.
Height	1 to 1½ feet. **Spread** 1 to 1½ feet.
Culture	*Low watering zones.* A little extra water in very dry weather promotes renewed blooming. Too much water tends to result in weak growth, and likely shortens the life of the plant. Good drainage is important. Plants will adapt to clay, but overwatering is a danger. In heavy grassland competition, plants can be quite small. In the open, they become almost shrub-like. Deadheading promotes continued blooming. Full sun. Expect seedlings.
Wildlife	Deer rarely, if ever, browse Mexican Hat Coneflower.
Natural Range	Southern Canada, Montana, and Minnesota, southward to Louisiana and Mexico.
Landscape Use	An attractive, showy plant for use singly or in large groups in gardens. A reliable, attractive plant for naturalizing in shortgrass, midgrass, and tallgrass meadows.
Propagation	Seed. No stratification needed. Will bloom the first year.
Notes	Generally, the color of the parent plant is the same as its seedlings, but it is not unusual to find plants with both red and yellow petals when there have been both red- and yellow-flowered plants in the garden.

SALVIA PITCHERI (syn. Salvia azurea var. grandiflora)

Pitcher Sage

Type of Plant	Long-lived perennial.
Flowers	Light blue clusters. September to October.
Height	3 to 4 feet. Occasionally to 6 feet. **Spread** About 3 feet.
Culture	*Low and moderate watering zones.* Grown dry, this plant is shorter and more attractive. With too much water, it grows very tall and sparse and may need staking. Pinching the tips one or more times up to mid-August will result in more flowers on shorter stems. Full sun.
Wildlife	Butterflies, bees, and moths love this plant. Monarch butterflies sometimes seek out this plant from others in the garden.
Natural Range	Minnesota and Nebraska, south to Arkansas and Texas. Naturalized in other areas.
Landscape Use	A beautiful blue addition to late summer and early fall gardens. Other plants can be grown close by to cover the bare lower part of the plant. An attractive addition to midgrass and tallgrass meadows.
Propagation	Seeds and cuttings. Germination is good with two-month stratification.
Notes	The U.S.D.A. Soil Conservation Service Plant Materials Center in Manhattan, Kansas, has released 'Nekan' Pitcher Sage for use in natural prairie restoration. 'Kaneb' Purple Prairie Clover (*Dalea purpurea var. 'kaneb'*) is another release from this center. It is reputed to bloom all summer and into the fall. This is significantly longer than many wild Purple Prairie Clover varieties that bloom for only one week.

SENECIO LONGILOBUS

Threadleaf Groundsel

Type of Plant	Long-lived perennial.
Flower	Numerous small, yellow daisies. September to October. A few flowers open occasionally through the summer.
Other Features	Attractive, silver foliage.
Height	1 to 2½ feet. **Spread** 2 to 2½ feet.
Culture	*Low watering zones.* Well-drained soil is best. Plants will adapt to clay if not overwatered. Too much water results in rampant sprawling growth. Cutting back the plant helps, and full bloom is still possible. Full sun.
Wildlife	Deer have so far completely avoided this plant, and it is reported to be toxic to cattle. Butterflies love it.
Natural Range	Colorado and Utah, south to Texas and Mexico.
Landscape Use	A very attractive addition to the fall garden color scheme. Useful singly or in midgrass and shortgrass meadows.
Propagation	Seed germinates well without stratification.
Notes	*Senecio spartioides* (Broom Groundsel) is similar, but is taller and narrower, with green foliage.

SILENE LACINIATA

Indian Pink, Catch Fly, Mexican Campion

Type of Plant	Long-lived perennial.
Flowers	Delightful, bright red trumpets with "ragged" edges. Late June into July, then off and on until freeze-up.
Height	1 to 1½ feet. **Spread** About 1 foot.
Culture	*Low watering zones.* Well-drained soil is best, although plants will adapt to clay if not overwatered. Deadheading will encourage a second bloom if plants have ceased flowering and have begun to set seed. No seedlings have been observed. Full sun.
Wildlife	Hummingbirds spend a surprisingly long time at each flower on this plant, suggesting large amounts of nectar, or very high quality nectar that is difficult to extract. As with several other hummingbird plants, this plant has red flowers and back-turned petals to encourage the birds while discouraging insects.
Natural Range	California to Texas, southward into Mexico.
Landscape Use	Very attractive used singly or in small groups in gardens. Because no seedlings have been observed in gardens, it is doubtful that this plant can be successfully naturalized in meadows. However, hand-planted individual plants would be attractive in shortgrass meadows.
Propagation	Seed. Germination is good after two months stratification.
Notes	Although this plant belongs to a family in which flower petals are separate, rather than fused into tubes suitable for hummingbird pollination, this particular species has evolved an ability to repel insects and attract hummingbirds by having petals that are confined within a tubular calyx.

STACHYS COCCINEA

Scarlet Hedgenettle

Type of Plant	Long-lived perennial.
Flowers	Brilliant scarlet, totally covering the plant at times. July to October.
Other Features	Fragrant foliage.
Height	1½ to 2 feet. **Spread** 1½ to 2 feet.
Culture	*Moderate and high watering zones.* This plant will adapt to less water, but seems to be at its best in rich, moist soil. It is somewhat marginal in hardiness when exposed to temperatures of less than –5°F. However, even one inch of snowcover has totally protected plants from more than 24 hours of –15°F temperatures. Blooming is "off and on" for much of the summer, with dramatic peaks. Deadheading helps renew blooming. Full sun is best, though light shade is acceptable.
Wildlife	The ultimate hummingbird plant! There have been many reports of hummingbirds commuting from the foothills to the far eastside suburbs of Denver for sips of Hedgenettle ambrosia.
Natural Range	Western Texas to southern Arizona, and into Mexico.
Landscape Use	A dazzling addition for moderate or high watering zones in flower gardens. Because it blooms into the fall, this plant should be good for attracting hummingbirds in Flagstaff, Albuquerque, and Santa Fe when the birds return from nesting in the central and northern Rockies. In Spokane or Boise, it may be possible to attract the aggressive rufous hummingbirds into gardens during the summer with Scarlet Hedgenettle.
Propagation	Seed germination has been difficult. Cuttings root well, if kept enclosed in plastic covers during the rooting period.
Notes	Scarlet Hedgenettle is another regional native plant that is little known in the commercial nursery trade, but which is worthy of widespread use in gardening. This is another plant that encourages hummingbird pollination and discourages insect pollination by having red flowers that birds see well but insects do not, by having flowers that butterflies can't perch on, by having back-turned petals that discourage crawling insects, and by avoiding insect-attracting fragrant flowers. No definitive theory has been discovered to explain why hummingbird pollination is favored by these plants, but several theories have been offered. For example, hummingbirds may pollinate over a larger area than insects, thus helping expand the range of the flowers. Or, hummingbirds may visit fewer species of flowers, thus improving the chances of the pollen getting to the "right" flowers. Or, the flowers may have evolved in response to a time when there was a relative shortage of pollinating insects. All of these theories have flaws, leaving the question open for further speculation. Is it possible that these plants simply don't like insects? Could these plants actually find insects "creepy"?

VERBENA BIPINNATIFIDA

Dakota Verbena

Type of Plant	Short-lived perennial, frequently winterkills the first year. This plant might be called a "perennial annual," returning each year as seedlings, or an "annual perennial" because it is supposed to be perennial, but seems to die every winter.
Flowers	Attractive lavender clusters. June until frost.
Height	About 12 inches. **Spread** About 2 feet.
Culture	*Low and moderate watering zones.* A little extra water in very dry weather will help sustain blooming. Well-drained soil is best. Full sun. Deadheading occasionally will promote continued blooming. Numerous seedlings are common.
Wildlife	The bright pink color is a favorite of butterflies, and the flat flower clusters make good landing surfaces for them. A few bees have developed special bristles on their front legs to aid in collecting pollen from plants like this. Rabbits are reported to be fond of some species of Verbena.
Natural Range	South Dakota to Alabama, west to Arizona and Mexico.
Landscape Use	An attractive, very showy groundcover for use singly or in groups. Also attractive in shortgrass meadows.
Propagation	Usually by seed. Stratification may help. Storage for a year or more may also help. May take several weeks for germination. Cuttings are reported to root well.
Notes	*Verbena tenera* and *Verbena tenuisecta* are excellent for low watering zone annual plantings in the Rocky Mountain region. *Verbena canadensis* is another attractive, usually short-lived species. Flowers are reddish-pink. Medicinally, verbenas are reported to be quite good at relieving early symptoms of colds and viruses. It is said to allay fevers, settle the stomach, and produce a general feeling of "relaxed well-being."

VIGUIERA MULTIFLORA

Showy Goldeneye

Type of Plant	Long-lived perennial.
Flowers	Delightful, yellow "daisies" totally covering the plant. June into October.
Height	To about 3 feet. **Spread** To about 3 feet.
Culture	*Low and moderate watering zones.* Too much water can kill the plants. Well-drained soil is important where too much water is likely to be a problem. Full sun. Dead-heading is usually not needed, but will renew blooming if plants decline. Expect numerous seedlings which generally germinate at one time and are easy to remove.
Wildlife	Bees and butterflies are common on this plant.
Natural Range	Montana to New Mexico and Arizona, Nevada, and eastern California.
Landscape Use	An extraordinarily showy plant. Very attractive as single plants, and good for naturalizing in tallgrass, midgrass, or shortgrass meadows.
Propagation	Seed. Very easy without stratification.
Notes	The name "Goldeneye" refers to the yellow flower centers. To bees, the flowers of Showy Goldeneye probably appear the way gaillardia looks to humans. Ultraviolet light likely creates a sharp contrast between the flower centers and petals.

ZAUSCHNERIA CALIFORNICA

California Zauschneria

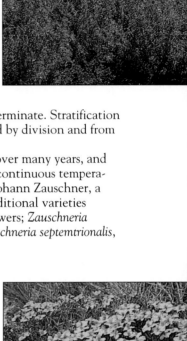

Type of Plant	Long-lived perennial.
Flowers	Bright red trumpets. Early fall. Timing of bloom is variable depending on the weather. Late September into October is common in Boulder, Denver, and Santa Fe.
Height	1 to 2 feet. **Spread** Variable to several feet.
Culture	*Low watering zones.* Plants will tolerate more water if drainage is good. Warm microclimates are helpful. Full sun.
Wildlife	Hummingbirds have usually migrated south of the central Rocky Mountain region before Zauschneria blooms. However, Santa Fe, Albuquerque, and Flagstaff are likely to see considerable hummingbird activity around this plant.
Natural Range	Primarily California.
Landscape Use	Attractive used either singly or in groups in gardens or shortgrass meadow areas.
Propagation	Seed. Warm conditions help. May take several months to germinate. Stratification probably not needed. Propagation can also be accomplished by division and from underground runners.
Notes	These plants have proved very hardy in Colorado gardens over many years, and have been known to survive exposure to several days with continuous temperatures between –15°F and –25°F. The species is named for Johann Zauschner, a professor of natural history at the University of Prague. Additional varieties include: *Zauschneria californica alba* , 8″x24″ with white flowers; *Zauschneria californica* 'Solidarity Pink,' 12″x24″ with pink flowers; *Zauschneria septemtrionalis*, 8″x18″, unusually low-growing with red flowers.

ZINNIA GRANDIFLORA

Prairie Zinnia

Type of Plant	Long-lived perennial.
Flowers	Bright yellow, daisy-like, totally covering the plants. June into October.
Other Features	The foliage is attractive.
Height	6 to 8 inches. **Spread** 10 inches or more (the plants tend to spread moderately by lateral rhizomes).
Culture	*Low watering zones.* Even moderate watering can be too much for this plant. Well-drained soil is important if too much water is likely to be a problem. Full sun.
Wildlife	Deer have not browsed this plant in several neighborhoods with large herds. Cattle also appear to avoid it.
Natural Range	Panhandles of Oklahoma and Texas, plus adjacent Colorado, Kansas, and New Mexico, southward into Mexico.
Landscape Use	A wonderful, drought-tolerant native for warm microclimates. Especially useful when allowed to develop into large patches. A good candidate for introduction into shortgrass meadows. Pregrown plants are likely to be more successful than trying to establish plants from seed in a meadow.
Propagation	Seed. Germination is somewhat low. Vernalization is not necessary.
Notes	Blooming can be somewhat erratic. Cutting around and into plants with a shovel has sometimes stimulated blooming. The genus is named for Johann Zinn, an 18th-century botanist who worked in New Mexico.

DECIDUOUS SHRUBS

AMORPHA CANESCENS

Leadplant

Type of Plant	Deciduous shrub.
Flowers	Blue spikes. July.
Other Features	Attractive gray foliage.
Height	To about 4 feet. **Spread** To about 4 feet.
Culture	*Low watering zones.* Adapts to a wide variety of soils, but good drainage is important if too much water is likely. Plants die back during the winter. Cutting them back in the fall helps overall appearance of the garden. Full sun.
Wildlife	Heavily grazed by cattle. This suggests that deer browsing might be a problem, though this has not been the case in several gardens with considerable numbers of deer.
Natural Range	Throughout the Great Plains.
Landscape Use	Because of its small size, it can be incorporated nicely into gardens. Also attractive as groups in shrub areas.
Propagation	Seed, probably with stratification.
Notes	*Amorpha nana* (Dwarf Leadplant) has green leaves and pink flowers. It grows to about two feet. It is easily propagated from seed stratified for about two months and does not die back during the winter. Dwarf Leadplant is found on scattered rocky hillsides over a wide area of the western Great Plains and adjacent foothills.

CHAMAEBATIARIA MILLEFOLIUM

Fernbush

Type of Plant	Semi-evergreen shrub. Technically this is an evergreen shrub, but in most of the region the leaves weather off during the winter and begin regrowing in very early spring.
Flowers	Attractive white, pointed clusters. July to August.
Other Features	Foliage is attractive through much of the year, even in colder areas. Foliage is fragrant.
Height	Usually 3 to 5 feet. **Spread** Usually 3 to 5 feet.
Culture	*Low watering zones.* Adapts to most soils, but well-drained soil is important if too much water is likely. Full sun. Trimming off seed heads after they have weathered considerably helps overall appearance.
Wildlife	Bees flock to the flowers. Deer are not known to browse this plant in gardens, but in range areas, browsing is reported.
Natural Range	Oregon to California, east to Arizona, Colorado, and Wyoming.
Landscape Use	A very showy plant when in bloom. Useful in areas that are difficult to water. An attractive background or accent in garden areas.
Propagation	Seeds. Three months stratification suggested.
Notes	This plant has not been well known in the nursery trade over most of the region, but it is gaining in popularity and availability.

CHRYSOTHAMNUS SPP.

Rabbitbrush

Type of Plant	Deciduous shrub.
Flowers	Spectacular yellow clusters. August into October, depending on the weather and the species.
Other Features	Foliage color varies from almost white to medium green. Stems have the same color as the leaves and add considerable color during the winter. Seed heads are often very ornamental.
Height	Variable with species and variety, from about 2 to 4 feet. **Spread** Variable from about 2 to 4 feet.
Culture	*Low watering zones.* Too much water produces "floppy" unattractive growth. Continuously wet soil often kills plants. Adapts to most soils if they are not too wet. Plants are usually more attractive if pruned back severely each fall, or before growth begins in the spring. This results in fuller plants and more blossoms. Full sun.
Wildlife	Deer have never been reported to browse on Rabbitbrush. Butterflies and bees flock to the flowers. Monarchs will sometimes concentrate on Rabbitbrush.
Natural Range	Many species and varieties have been identified by various botanists. One or more of these can be found over most of western North America.
Landscape Use	A very attractive addition to flower gardens. Winter seed heads and twigs add considerable interest during the time when herbaceous plants have died back to ground level. Also useful in large shrub masses in residential, park, and commercial landscaping.
Propagation	Usually by seed. No stratification required. Fresh seed is best. Also by cuttings.
Notes	From the numerous and confusing species and varieties reported by various botanists, the following characteristics are most useful in landscaping: 1. full-size (3 to 4 feet) with blue or green foliage, 2. dwarf size (1½ to 2 feet) with blue or green foliage, 3. early and late blooming varieties of dwarf, full-size, and blue or green varieties. Native Americans used the flexible branches in basketmaking. A yellow dye has been made from the flower heads. When twigs and leaves are added, a soft olive-green color is produced. In the Great Basin area, a chewing gum was created from the roots. This plant rarely, if ever, invades rangeland. However, because cattle avoid Rabbitbrush, it rapidly increases on overgrazed ranges. The word "*Chrysothamnus*" comes from the Greek words *chryso* for golden and *thamnus* for bush.

FALLUGIA PARADOXA

Apache Plume

Type of Plant	Deciduous shrub.
Flowers	White, like small single roses. June, then off and on until late fall.
Other Features	Very interesting and decorative seed plumes.
Height	Usually 3 to 5 feet. **Spread** Usually 3 to 5 feet.
Culture	*Low watering zones.* Most soil is suitable, but in clay overwatering can be a problem. Sometimes several years are needed for establishment. In very dry situations, several deep waterings during the summer will sustain blooming. No pruning necessary. A few suckers can be expected, but invasiveness is not a problem. Full sun.
Wildlife	Deer browsing has not been observed in landscape situations, but is reported occasionally in range country.
Natural Range	California, Nevada, Utah, Colorado, south into Mexico.
Landscape Use	Quite ornamental, especially when the seeds are backlighted by the sun. Very useful in dry, hot, sunny locations. Attractive as single accent plants in flower gardens, or in shrub plantings with a few flowers for extra color.
Propagation	Seed. Stratification not necessary. Germination is somewhat erratic. Cuttings, layering, and root division are other methods of propagation.
Notes	Native Americans were known to use the stems as brooms and arrow shafts. A brew from the leaves was believed to promote hair growth.

ROSA GLAUCA (syn. Rosa rubrifolia)

Redleaf Rose

Type of Plant	Deciduous shrub.
Flowers	Pink. Single. Spring.
Other Features	Attractive reddish foliage and ornamental red rose hips. Foliage is more gray-green if grown in light shade. Branches arch outward very attractively.
Height	Usually 5 to 10 feet. **Spread** Usually 5 to 8 feet.
Culture	*Moderate watering zones.* This plant will tolerate both more and less water. It will do well in dry, light shade, and it will grow well in most soils.
Wildlife	Deer severely browse this plant if it is grown in wet rich soil. If grown dry, browsing is significantly reduced.
Natural Range	Central European Mountains from the Pyrenees to Poland, Romania, and Albania.
Landscape Use	A very attractive accent shrub for full sun or part shade. Relatively few thorns make this rose easier to work around in a flower garden setting than many others.
Propagation	Usually grown from seed.
Notes	Most roses are quite drought-tolerant. Many will grow well in considerably drier conditions than the moderate watering zones defined in this book. Deer browsing is a serious problem with most roses. As with *Rosa glauca*, other roses are browsed much less when they are grown dry. Rose hips are an important source of vitamin C.

EVERGREEN SHRUBS

ARTEMISIA TRIDENTATA

Big Western Sage

Type of Plant	Semi-evergreen shrub.
Flowers	Relatively insignificant.
Other Features	Very attractive, fragrant foliage.
Height	Variable, but commonly 3 to 4 feet. **Spread** 3 to 4 feet.
Culture	*Moderate watering zones.* Adapts to more or less water and most soils, but on clay overwatering is a potential problem. Occasional pruning will result in more foliage and more compact plants. Full sun.
Wildlife	Deer have not browsed this sage in several landscapes with large deer herds. Browsing is reported in range country, however.
Natural Range	Canada to Texas, west to Cascades and Sierra Nevadas.
Landscape Use	A very attractive addition to gardens as an accent plant, or in background masses.
Propagation	Usually by seed.

Verbena tenera, V. tenuisecta

Notes *Artemisia* comes from Artemis, the Greek goddess of the moon, wild places, and wild animals. Native Americans are said to have mitigated the effects of skunk encounters with smoke from burning *Artemisia tridentata.* Powdered leaves were also used as a remedy for "diaper rash." The entire plant is considered to be anti-microbial. The French refer to various *artemisias* as *garde robe*, a reference to their insect repelling properties.

COWANIA MEXICANA
(syn. Cowania mexicana var. stansburiana, Cowania stansburiana, Purshia mexicana)

Cowania or Cliffrose

Type of Plant	Broadleaf evergreen shrub.
Flowers	Showy, fragrant, light yellow. Off and on June to fall.
Other Features	Picturesque, irregular shape and evergreen foliage.
Height	Variable, but usually 5 to 15 feet. **Spread** 3 to 5 feet.
Culture	*Low watering zones.* Well-drained sandy or gravelly soil is best, but clay is satisfactory if not overwatered. Too much water results in rampant, unattractive growth and possible loss of plants. Plants can be pruned severely to shape them. Full sun.
Wildlife	To date there are no reports of landscape plants being browsed, but in range country browsing is reported.
Natural Range	Utah, Arizona, Colorado, and New Mexico.
Landscape Use	Because of its unusual, open form, enough light penetrates this shrub to allow many herbaceous flowers to grow nearby. The shape, fragrant flowers, and evergreen foliage make this an attractive shrub for flower garden areas.
Propagation	Seeds. Early season seeds best. Two to 3 months stratification helps germination.
Notes	*Stansburiana,* one of several variety (or species) names for this plant, refers to an English merchant who introduced a number of native American plants to England.

EPHEDRA VIRIDIS, EPHEDRA TORREYANA, and EPHEDRA NEVADENSIS

Green Ephedra, Torrey Ephedra, and Nevada Ephedra

Type of Plant	Evergreen shrubs.
Flowers	Staminate (pollen-bearing) flowers can be quite attractive. Late spring. Pistillate (seed-bearing) flowers are on separate plants.
Other Features	Fruits form on pistillate plants and are quite attractive in most cases. It is the year-round colorful stems, however, that are the major ornamental feature.
Height	Usually 1 to 3 feet. **Spread** Usually 1 to 3 feet.
Culture	*Low watering zones.* Well-drained soil, or clay that is not overwatered. Full sun.
Wildlife	Quail, antelope, and ground squirrels eat the seeds. Wild and domestic animals are reported to browse on the stems, though deer have noticeably avoided *E. viridis* and *E. nevadensis* in some landscape settings.

E. viridis and Shepherdia rotundifolia

Natural Range	*E. viridis:* New Mexico, western Colorado, Utah, Arizona, and California. *E. torreyana:* Nevada, Utah, western Colorado, Arizona, New Mexico, and Mexico. *E. nevadensis:* Nevada, Utah, California, northwestern Arizona.
Landscape Use	Very interesting small shrubs. The colorful, evergreen stems add interest during the time of the year when most herbaceous plants have died back to the ground.
Propagation	Seed. All of the Ephedras require only a brief period of stratification (1–2 weeks), if any at all, and the germination rate is generally quite high.
Notes	Additional species of ornamental interest include *Ephedra minima, E. minuta, E. gerardiana,* and *E. Americana* var. *andina.*

MAHONIA FREMONTII and MAHONIA HAEMATOCARPA

Fremont and Redberry Mahonia

Type of Plant	Evergreen shrub.
Flowers	Attractive yellow clusters with pleasant light fragrance. Mid-spring. Time of bloom varies greatly with the location and the species.
Other Features	Fruit: *M. fremontii,* dark blue berries. *M. haematocarpa,* red berries.
Height	Usually 5 to 6 feet. **Spread** Usually 5 to 6 feet.
Culture	*Low and moderate watering zones.* Well-drained soil. Full sun is best for these species.
Wildlife	Deer browsing is very unlikely because of the very sharp, prickly leaves on these species.
Natural Range	*M. fremontii:* the Four Corners area. *M. haematocarpa:* central and southern Arizona and New Mexico.
Landscape Use	Interesting evergreen shrubs with attractive fragrant flowers and prickly foliage.
Propagation	Seed. Stratification for several months helps. Cleaning all fruit off the seeds is helpful. If fruit is dried, puncturing the dried skin helps. Propagation from stem cuttings and roots is also reported possible.

ORNAMENTAL GRASSES

ANDROPOGON SCOPARIUS

Little Bluestem

Type of Plant	A perennial warm season bunch grass.
Flowers	Relatively inconspicuous.
Other Features	Attractive seed heads develop in early fall about the time the entire plant becomes a beautiful reddish-brown.
Height	2 to 3 feet. **Spread** 1 to 2 feet.
Culture	*Low and moderate watering zones.* Most soils. Full sun.
Wildlife	An important butterfly larval host plant.
Natural Range	Southern Canada, Maine to Idaho, south to Florida, and Arizona into Mexico.
Landscape Use	An attractive clump grass for accent in flower gardens and a good grass for midgrass meadows because it naturally spaces itself, leaving room for wildflowers.
Propagation	Seed. Very good germination has resulted from two months stratification.
Notes	This was one of the major native grasses of the Great Plains that supported vast herds of buffalo and pronghorns, and later the domestic cattle industry. It is currently being used in western roadside restoration.

BOUTELOUA CURTIPENDULA

Sideoats Grama

Type of Plant	A warm season perennial bunch grass.
Flowers	Ornamentally insignificant.
Other Features	Very attractive seeds arranged on opposite sides of a zigzag stem. The entire plant becomes an attractive tan color in the fall.
Height	Usually 1 to 3 feet. **Spread** Usually less than 1 foot.
Culture	*Moderate and low watering zones.* Any soil. Full sun.
Wildlife	A very important forage plant for all grazing animals. An important butterfly larval host plant.
Natural Range	Everywhere in the continental United States except the extreme Northwest and Southwest. A major component of the central and southern Great Plains grasslands.
Landscape Use	A very attractive mid-height grass for accent in flower gardens, and an excellent major component of midgrass wildflower meadows.
Propagation	Seed. Two months stratification has resulted in very good germination.
Notes	Bunch grasses like Sideoats Grama make good components of wildflower meadows because they leave space for the wildflowers. Bunch grasses are typically found on drier sites than sod forming grasses. Buffalo grass (*Buchloë dactyloides*) is an exception. Generally, as prevailing conditions get drier, the grasses are shorter, and the spaces between bunches become greater.

KOELERIA CRISTATA (syn. Koeleria pyramidata)

Junegrass

Type of Plant	A cool season perennial bunch grass.
Flowers	Showy, long, narrow panicles. June.
Other Features	Attractive green foliage clump.
Height	6 to 12 inches. **Spread** About 6 inches.
Culture	*Low and moderate watering zones.* Any soil. Full sun.
Wildlife	This is considered one of the important grasses that serve as larval host plants for many butterflies, including all Skippers and most Browns and Satyrs.
Natural Range	Throughout the temperate Northern Hemisphere.
Landscape Use	An attractive small clump grass. Similar to the more familiar Blue Fescue (*Festuca glauca*). The flowers are very attractive.
Propagation	Very easy from field-collected seed. Stratification not necessary.
Notes	Before the introduction of domestic wheat, Pueblo Indians in New Mexico reportedly made both bread and a mush from the seeds of this grass.

SORGHASTRUM NUTANS

Indiangrass

Type of Plant	A warm season perennial bunch grass.
Flowers	Attractive long, narrow panicles. Late summer.
Other Features	The seed heads are quite attractive, and the entire plant turns a beautiful reddish-orange color in the fall.
Height	Usually to 5 feet. **Spread** 1 to 3 feet.
Culture	*Moderate watering zones.* Most soils. Full sun.
Wildlife	A very important grass for cattle forage. Probably formerly an important grass for Great Plains buffalo.
Natural Range	Quebec to Manitoba, south to Florida and Arizona into Mexico.
Landscape Use	A very useful plant for striking accent in flower gardens.
Propagation	Seed. Stratification for two months has resulted in good germination.
Notes	This is one of about ten major grasses of the productive original tallgrass prairies of the eastern Great Plains.

GRAY WATER FOR GARDENING

As water shortages become really serious, it becomes increasingly attractive to consider using the water from showers, bathtubs, bathroom sinks, and washing machines to help save landscaping. This "gray water" can exceed 100 gallons per person per week, with washing machines alone contributing 35 to 70 gallons per load.

Acceptable Uses

The California Department of Health Services considers water from bathtubs, showers, bathroom sinks, and washing machines (excluding diaper loads) to be acceptable for some uses. Water from kitchen sinks and dishwashers, however, is likely to have too much food and grease to be used without trouble. Ornamental and fruit trees, shrubs, flowers, groundcovers and lawns (if people will not be in contact with them) can be irrigated safely with this gray water.

Unacceptable Uses

Gray water should not come in contact with edible parts of food crops, and gray water should not be used for below-ground crops like carrots, beets, and potatoes.

Are Soaps and Detergents Good or Bad?

Generally, soaps are less troublesome than detergents, but both can cause problems if used extensively over long periods. One of the problems are the sodium salts in many of these products. Detergents advertised as having special "softening powers" or "enzyme actions" are likely to be worse than others. Be cautious about using water from laundry loads with bleach, and avoid products with boron. The phosphates in detergents, however, are actually considered helpful, and it is reported that surface tension reducing ingredients may help water penetrate "tight" clay soils. Water from household water softeners should be avoided because of the potential for excessive sodium in the water.

Methods of Application

Drip irrigation methods are acceptable. Spray application is not considered acceptable because of the potential of inhaling contaminated water, and because it is very difficult to direct the water with adequate precision.

Regulation of Gray Water Use

Communities vary greatly in governing gray water use, with plumbing codes in many places specifically prohibiting permanent gray water plumbing. This is changing fast, however, so it is best to consult local agencies.

Sources
The Integral Urban House: Self-Reliant Living in the City. Olkowski, Javits, and Farallones Institute, Sierra Club Books, 1979.
Sunset magazine, "Drought Survival Guide for Home and Garder," May 1991.

APPENDIX
Additional
Resources

❀ *Blooming Sequence of*
  Selected Waterwise Flowers

❀ *Meadow Mixes*
  Butterfly, Hummingbird, Tallgrass,
  Midgrass, Shortgrass

❀ *Wildlife Plant Lists*
  Hummingbird Plants, Butterfly Plants,
  Deer-resistant Plants

❀ *Eating Your Yard*

❀ *Grasses for Waterwise Lawns*

❀ *Sources of Plants*

❀ *Public Xeriscape Demonstration Areas*

❀ *Organizations of Interest*

❀ *Annotated Bibliography*
  Horticulture and Design,
  Xeriscape, Wildlife Gardening,
  Natural and Cultural History,
  Edible Landscaping ∎

Blooming Sequence of Selected Waterwise Flowers

The typical blooming times and blooming sequence for some selected waterwise flowers are given in these charts for Boulder, Colorado, and Flagstaff, Arizona. Although the sequence of bloom remains fairly consistent throughout the Rocky Mountain region, altitude (and consequently prevailing temperature) varies considerably. Generally, lower areas are warmer and have earlier blooming times than higher areas, which are typically cooler. However, a few species seem to prefer relatively cool weather when they bloom, and sometimes bloom for a longer period when it is cool. Wild White Yarrow (*Achillea lanulosa*), for example, appears to demonstrate this by blooming longer in Flagstaff than in Boulder, where it tends to be warmer when this yarrow blooms. Conversely, some heat-loving plants, such as Chocolate Flower (*Berlandiera lyrata*), seem to bloom better in Boulder than in Flagstaff because it is warmer in the summer in Boulder.

MORE MONARCH MYSTIQUE

Monarch butterflies are defended from predation by birds because glycoside chemicals they consume from eating milkweed plants makes them distasteful to the birds. This form of protection has been so successful that the very edible viceroy butterfly has evolved to mimic the appearance of the monarch in order to protect itself.

A report in an April 1991 issue of the British journal *Nature* sheds new light on this long-held belief, however. In this study, sixteen wild blackbirds were fed viceroy, monarch, and queen butterflies. Abdomens were used so that wing patterns would not affect the choices. Birds that tasted viceroys showed noticeable distress.

The new puzzle is: if viceroys are not trying to protect a tasty body, why do they look so much like monarchs? One of the researchers commented, "It still pays them to mutually advertise. . . ." If they evolve to look alike, each species is likely to lose fewer individuals before predators learn not to eat them. ∎

BLOOMING SEQUENCE

Selected Waterwise Flowers and Shrubs, Boulder, Colorado*

Plant Name	April	May	June	July	Aug.	Sep.	Oct.
Tulipa turkestanica	■						
Iris bucharica	■						
Aurinia saxatilis		■					
Phlox subulata		■					
Tulipa linifolia		■					
Delosperma nubigenum			■				
Linum perenne var. lewisii			■	■	■		
Cerastium tomentosum			■	■			
Anacyclus depressus			■				
Penstemon virens			■				
Penstemon secundiflorus			■				
Penstemon linarioides			■				
Chrysanthemum leucanthemum			■				
Phlox nana			■	■	■		
Penstemon crandallii			■				
Penstemon pinifolius			■	■			
Achillea ageratifolia			■	■			
Iris (bearded)			■				
Thymus (lemon)			■				
Salvia officinalis			■				
Penstemon strictus			■				
Koeleria cristata			■				
Berlandiera lyrata			■	■	■	■	■
Penstemon alpinus			■				
Delosperma cooperi			■	■	■	■	■
Achillea × 'Moonshine'			■	■			
Cowania mexicana			■	■			
Psilostrophe tagetina			■	■	■	■	
Penstemon neo-mexicanus				■			
Callirhoe involucrata			■	■	■	■	■
Oenothera missouriensis			■	■			
Digitalis lanata			■	■	■		
Fallugia paradoxa			■	■			
Viguiera multiflora			■	■	■	■	
Townsendia grandiflora			■	■			
Epilobium angustifolium			■	■	■		
Gaillardia aristata			■	■	■		
Senecio longilobus			■	■	■		
Achillea lanulosa			■	■			
Penstemon cobaea			■				
Silene laciniata			■	■	■	■	
Ratibida columnifera			■	■	■	■	
Santolina spp.				■			
Lavandula spp.				■	■		
Coreopsis lanceolata			■	■	■		
Centranthus ruber			■	■	■	■	
Penstemon murrayanus				■	■		
Penstemon barbatus			■	■			
Monarda fistulosa				■			
Amorpha canescens				■			
Rudbeckia hirta				■	■	■	■

Plant Name	April	May	June	July	Aug.	Sep.	Oct.
Echinacea purpurea				▓	▓		
Anthemis tinctoria				▓	▓	▓	▓
Perovskia atriplicifolia				▓	▓	▓	▓
Penstemon kunthii				▓	▓	▓	▓
Stachys coccinea				▓	▓	▓	▓
Achillea × 'Coronation Gold'				▓	▓	▓	
Dalea purpurea				▓	▓		
Zinnia grandiflora				▓	▓	▓	
Caryopteris × clandonensis					▓	▓	
Chamaebatiaria millefolium					▓		
Eustoma grandiflorum					▓	▓	▓
Melampodium leucanthum					▓	▓	▓
Sphaeralcea spp.					▓	▓	
Verbena bipinnatifida					▓	▓	▓
Talinum calycinum					▓	▓	
Abronia fragrans					▓	▓	
Lobelia siphilitica					▓	▓	
Oenothera caespitosa					▓	▓	
Senecio longilobus					▓	▓	
Chrysothamnus sp. (green)						▓	
Liatris punctata						▓	
Gutierrezia sarothrae						▓	▓
Salvia pitcheri						▓	▓
Helianthus maximiliani						▓	
Zauschneria californica						▓	
Chrysothamnus sp. (silver)						▓	
Agastache cana						▓	▓

*The site on which this information was recorded is somewhat cooler than most of the metro Denver area. Therefore, some of the plants tend to bloom several weeks later on this site.

BLOOMING SEQUENCE

Selected Waterwise Flowers and Shrubs, Flagstaff, Arizona*

Plant Name	April	May	June	July	Aug.	Sep.	Oct.
Mahonia repens		●					
Geum triflorum		●	●				
Iris reticulata	●	●					
Aquilegia elegantula		●	●				
Phlox subulata		●	●				
Prunus besseyi		●	●				
Potentilla fruticosa			●	●	●	●	●
Achillea lanulosa			●	●	●	●	
Aquilegia chrysantha			●	●	●		
Chrysanthemum leucanthemum			●	●	●	●	
Gypsophila repens			●	●	●		
Penstemon crandallii			●	●			
Linum perenne var. lewisii			●	●	●	●	
Aquilegia caerulea			●	●	●		
Penstemon eatonii			●	●	●		
Penstemon gormanii			●	●			
Penstemon whippleanus				●	●	●	
Penstemon linarioides				●	●	●	●
Penstemon pinifolius				●	●	●	
Penstemon pseudospectabilis				●	●		
Penstemon strictus			●	●			
Kniphofia uvaria				●	●		
Saponaria ocymoides			●	●			
Achillea tomentosa			●	●			
Campanula rotundifolia			●	●	●	●	
Eriogonum umbellatum			●	●			
Gaillardia aristata			●	●	●	●	
Gilia aggregata			●	●	●		
Centranthus ruber				●	●	●	
Geranium caespitosum				●	●		
Penstemon barbatus				●	●		
Penstemon grandiflorus				●			
Ratibida columnifera				●	●		
Thymus × citroidorus				●	●		
Digitalis lutea				●	●		
Monarda fistulosa				●	●	●	
Oxytropis lambertii				●	●	●	
Silene laciniata				●	●	●	
Coreopsis lanceolata				●	●	●	
Coreopsis verticillata				●	●	●	
Dalea purpurea				●	●	●	
Echinacea purpurea				●	●	●	
Chamaebatiaria millefolium				●	●	●	
Teucrium chamaedrys				●	●	●	
Buddleia davidii					●	●	
Penstemon murrayanus					●		
Chrysothamnus spp.						●	
Helianthus maximiliani						●	●

*This information is from the Arboretum at Flagstaff, which is located in an area colder than most of the Flagstaff area. It is often 10–12°F colder than central Flagstaff, while the east side of town is often 10–12° warmer than central Flagstaff during winter nights.

MEADOW MIXES

Butterflies, Hummingbirds, Tallgrass, Midgrass, Shortgrass

These mixes are offered as a guide (rather than a formula) for developing attractive meadows. The ratio of species in the mixes has been left for the individual gardener to determine, because gardeners will have different preferences and because growing conditions will vary on different sites. Most species are native to the Rocky Mountain region. There are a few introduced species, however, and these are indicated for the convenience of those wishing to create purely "native" meadows.

HUMMINGBIRD MEADOW MIX

Moderate Watering Zones

This mix includes plants that have proved very attractive to hummingbirds in Boulder, Colorado.

Agastache cana	Double Bubble Mint
Andropogon scoparius	Little Bluestem
Berlandiera lyrata	Chocolate Flower
Bouteloua curtipendula	Sideoats Grama
Chrysanthemum leucanthemum	Ox-eye Daisy
Gilia aggregata	Scarlet Gilia
Helianthus maximiliani	Maximilian's Sunflower
Penstemon secundiflorus	Sidebells Penstemon
Penstemon barbatus	Scarlet Bugler
Viguiera multiflora	Showy Goldeneye

BUTTERFLY MEADOW MIX

Moderate Watering Zones

The plants in this mix have been very successful in attracting butterflies in Boulder, Colorado.

Andropogon scoparius	Little Bluestem
Berlandiera lyrata	Chocolate Flower
Bouteloua curtipendula	Sideoats Grama
Echinacea purpurea	Purple Coneflower
Gaillardia aristata	Gaillardia, Indian Blanket
Helianthus maximiliani	Maximilian's Sunflower
Ratibida columnifera	Mexican Hat Coneflower
Salvia pitcheri	Pitcher Sage
Senecio longilobus	Threadleaf Groundsel
Viguiera multiflora	Showy Goldeneye

TALLGRASS MEADOW MIX

This mix is generally best suited to moderate watering zone conditions. Especially at lower elevations, and in the southern parts of the region, this mix will require irrigation.

GRASSES

Andropogon gerardii	Big Bluestem
Panicum virgatum	Switchgrass
Sorghastrum nutans	Indiangrass

WILDFLOWERS

Achillea lanulosa	Native White Yarrow
Chrysanthemum leucanthemum	Ox-eye Daisy (introduced from Eurasia)
Echinacea purpurea	Purple Coneflower
Gaillardia aristata	Gaillardia, Indian Blanket
Helianthus maximiliani	Maximilian's Sunflower
Linum perenne var. *lewisii*	Lewis' Flax
Monarda fistulosa	Wild Monarda
Salvia pitcheri	Pitcher Sage
Viguiera multiflora	Showy Goldeneye

MIDGRASS MEADOW MIX

This mix is also likely to require some irrigation in many parts of the Rocky Mountain region. Note that Crested Wheatgrass is not a native species in this region, but it is very attractive, and has become well established.

GRASSES

Agropyron cristatum	Crested Wheatgrass
Andropogon scoparius	Little Bluestem
Bouteloua curtipendula	Sideoats Grama

WILDFLOWERS

Achillea lanulosa	Native White Yarrow
Agastache cana	Double Bubble Mint
Berlandiera lyrata	Chocolate Flower
Chrysanthemum leucanthemum	Ox-eye Daisy (introduced from Eurasia)
Dalea purpurea	Purple Prairie Clover
Gaillardia aristata	Gaillardia, Indian Blanket
Gilia aggregata	Scarlet Gilia
Linum perenne var. *lewisii*	Lewis' Flax
Mirabilis multiflora	Wild Four O'Clock
Monarda fistulosa	Wild Monarda
Penstemon secundiflorus	Sidebells Penstemon
Ratibida columnifera	Mexican Hat Coneflower

Salvia pitcheri	Pitcher Sage
Senecio longilobus	Threadleaf Groundsel
Senecio spartioides	Broom Groundsel
Viguiera multiflora	Showy Goldeneye

SHORTGRASS MEADOW MIX

This mix will rarely need irrigation anywhere in the region. In fact, if given too much water, taller, cool season plants will invade it. Note that Buffalograss is a very aggressive competitor, especially on clay soil. If wildflowers are the primary interest, consideration should be given to omitting this grass.

GRASSES

Bouteloua gracilis	Blue Grama
Buchloë dactyloides	Buffalograss

WILDFLOWERS

Berlandiera lyrata	Chocolate Flower
Chrysopsis spp.	Golden Asters
Gaillardia aristata	Gaillardia, Indian Blanket
Gilia aggregata	Scarlet Gilia
Gutierrezia sarothrae	Snakeweed
Liatris punctata	Dotted Gayfeather
Linum perenne var. lewisii	Lewis' Flax
Melampodium leucanthum	Blackfoot Daisy
Mirabilis multiflora	Wild Four O'Clock
Penstemon secundiflorus	Sidebells Penstemon
Psilostrophe tagetina	Paperflower
Ratibida columnifera	Mexican Hat Coneflower
Senecio longilobus	Threadleaf Groundsel
Senecio spartioides	Broom Groundsel
Silene laciniata	Indian Pink
Verbena bipinnatifida	Dakota Verbena
Viguiera multiflora	Showy Goldeneye
Zinnia grandiflora	Prairie Zinnia

WILDLIFE PLANT LISTS

Hummingbird Plants, Butterfly Plants, & Deer-resistant Plants

HUMMINGBIRD PLANTS

The plants in this list have proved to be big favorites of hummingbirds in the Denver-Boulder area. Using plants from the list, it is possible to have flowers blooming from the beginning to the end of the local hummingbird season. Some of the plants will be attractive to hummingbirds in all parts of the Rocky Mountain region. In other areas, however, hummingbirds may not be present at the time the flowers are in bloom. Experimentation will be necessary in areas considerably distant from the Boulder-Denver area.

FLOWERS

Agastache cana	Double Bubble Mint
Epilobium angustifolium	Fireweed
Gilia aggregata	Scarlet Gilia
Monarda didyma 'Cambridge Scarlet'	Cambridge Scarlet Monarda
Penstemon barbatus	Scarlet Bugler
Penstemon eatonii	Eaton's Penstemon
Penstemon kunthii	Kunthii Penstemon
Penstemon murrayanus	Murray's Penstemon
Penstemon pinifolius	Pineleaf Penstemon
Silene laciniata	Indian Pink
Stachys coccinea*	Scarlet Hedgenettle

VINES

Campsis radicans	Trumpet Creeper
Lonicera sempervirens	Scarlet Trumpet Honeysuckle

*Note: this may be the ultimate hummingbird plant.

BUTTERFLY PLANTS

In the Boulder-Denver area of Colorado, butterflies have shown special interest in these plants, though almost any showy plant will attract some butterflies.

FLOWERS

Asclepias tuberosa	Butterfly Weed
Echinacea purpurea	Purple Coneflower
Gaillardia aristata	Gaillardia, Indian Blanket
Helianthus maximiliani	Maximilian's Sunflower
Hemerocallis spp.	Daylilies
Perovskia atriplicifolia	Russian Sage
Salvia pitcheri*	Pitcher Sage
Senecio longilobus	Threadleaf Groundsel

*Note: monarchs like this plant especially well.

SHRUBS

Buddleia davidii	Butterfly Bush
Caryopteris x clandonensis	Bluemist Spirea
Chrysothamnus spp.*	Rabbitbrush

*Note: this plant is a favorite with monarchs.

DEER-RESISTANT PLANTS

The way in which plants are grown is one of the most significant factors determining whether they are browsed. For example, plants that are heavily fertilized and watered are eaten considerably more frequently than plants that are grown on natural precipitation, without fertilizer.

It is also important to note that browsing behavior of deer is extremely variable over time even in one locale. When comparing browsing behavior over great geographic distances, even more variability can be expected. However, because the plants in this list have survived well with the high deer population in Boulder, Colorado, they offer a good gamble for gardeners throughout the Rocky Mountain states.

FLOWERS

Achillea lanulosa	Native White Yarrow
Achillea filipendulina var.	Yarrow varieties
Agastache cana	Double Bubble Mint
Berlandiera lyrata	Chocolate Flower
Cerastium tomentosum	Snow-in-Summer
Chrysanthemum leucanthemum	Ox-eye Daisy
Chrysopsis spp.	Golden Aster species
Coreopsis spp.	Coreopsis species
Dalea purpurea	Purple Prairie Clover
Delphinium spp.	Delphinium species
Digitalis lanata	Grecian Foxglove
Echinacea purpurea	Purple Coneflower
Euphorbia myrsinites	Myrtle Euphorbia
Gaillardia aristata	Gaillardia, Indian Blanket
Geranium spp.	Hardy Geraniums
Gutierrezia sarothrae	Snakeweed
Gypsophila spp.	Baby's Breath
Helianthus maximiliani	Maximilian's Sunflower
Helleborus spp.	Hellebore species
Hemerocallis spp.	Daylilies
Iris spp.	Iris species
Kniphofia spp.	Poker Plant species
Liatris punctata	Gayfeathers
Melampodium leucanthum	Blackfoot Daisy
Mentha spp.	Mint species

FLAGSTAFF HUMMINGBIRD NOTES

The Arboretum at Flagstaff, Arizona, reports that a large number of broad-tailed hummingbirds pass through the area in the spring, and again in the fall, with some remaining to breed in the summer. Rufous hummingbirds (sometimes called Red Baron hummingbirds for their aggressiveness) pass through quickly in the spring, and show up again in early July; then stay until the weather drives them farther south. Anna's hummingbirds in this area are found mostly outside the city of Flagstaff. Calliope hummingbirds are quite rare, and black-chinned hummers are more common in nearby Sedona, which is at a lower elevation.

Red-flowered *Penstemon barbatus* is a favorite of local hummingbirds, but blue-flowered *Penstemon strictus* will be visited, apparently as a second choice. *Salvia lemmonii* (from about 9,000 feet on Mt. Lemon near Tucson) is being experimented with for winter hardiness, and seems to be another good plant for hummingbirds. *Zauschneria californica* has been successful only in a sheltered location at the arboretum, so it seems to be of limited value for late-season hummingbirds. ■

Mertensia spp.	Mertensia species
Mirabilis multiflora	Wild Four O'Clock
Monarda fistulosa	Wild Monarda
Narcissus spp.	Daffodils
Oenothera missouriensis	Ozark Evening Primrose
Origanum spp.	Oregano species
Origanum spp.	Marjoram species
Paeonia spp.	Peony species
Penstemon spp. *	Penstemon species
Perovskia atriplicifolia	Russian Sage
Phlox subulata	Creeping Phlox
Psilostrophe tagetina	Paperflower
Ratibida columnifera	Mexican Hat Coneflower
Rheum spp.	Rhubarb species
Rudbeckia hirta	Gloriosa Daisy
Salvia officinalis	Cooking Sage
Santolina chamaecyparissus	Santolina
Senecio longilobus	Threadleaf Groundsel
Senecio spartioides	Broom Groundsel
Silene laciniata	Indian Pink
Solidago spp.	Goldenrod species
Sphaeralcea spp.	Globemallow species
Thermopsis spp.	Goldenbanner species
Thymus spp.	Thyme species
Viguiera multiflora	Showy Goldeneye
Zauschneria spp.	Zauschneria species
Zinnia grandiflora	Prairie Zinnia

*Note: penstemons vary in palatability to deer.

SHRUBS

Amorpha canescens	Leadplant
Amorpha nana	Dwarf Leadplant
Artemisia abrotanum	Southernwood
Artemisia tridentata	Big Western Sage
Atriplex canescens	Four-wing Saltbush
Caryopteris × clandonensis	Bluemist Spirea
Cercocarpus ledifolius	Curlleaf Mountain Mahogany
Chamaebatiaria millefolium	Fernbush
Chrysothamnus spp.	Rabbitbrush species
Cotoneaster spp.	Cotoneaster species
Cowania mexicana	Cowania
Euonymus alata	Burning Bush
Fallugia paradoxa	Apache Plume
Mahonia repens	Creeping Mahonia
Pinus edulis	Piñon Pine
Potentilla fruticosa	Potentilla
Spiraea spp.	Spirea species

EATING YOUR YARD

Waterwise Edible Landscaping

Yes, it is possible to combine both water-efficient gardening and edible landscaping in the Rocky Mountain region. This drawing shows some of the ways to do it. Many of the edible plants (especially the shrubs, trees, and vines) simply require less water than most traditional landscape plants. Even water-demanding plants such as lettuce, however, are part of an overall water conservation strategy if they replace purely ornamental water-thirsty plants.

One good method to study incorporating edible plantings into an existing design, or a new design being developed, is to overlay a sketch or drawing of the area being studied with tracing paper. On the tracing paper, various substitute plants can be considered for sun, shade, appearance, and water requirements. This technique is also useful when refining a design for wildlife plantings. See the lists on the following pages for suggestions for edible plants and their relative water requirements.

Edible Plants: A Word to the Wise

"Learning taxonomy by taste," as one plantsman in Utah put it, can lead to serious consequences. Virginia Creeper (*Parthenocissus quinquefolia*), for example, can create crystals and severe irritation in the digestive system of humans.

It is important to know exactly what plant is about to be tasted, as well as whether it is entirely safe—sometimes one part of a plant is ok, and another part is not. It is also important to know whether the plant has been sprayed with any harmful chemicals. When reading about ethnobotanical uses of plants, bear in mind that special treatment may be involved, and using proper amounts of various ingredients can be critical.

Fortunately, serious poisoning from either wild plants or landscape plants is quite rare. This is probably based on the fact that most people are naturally cautious, as well as the fact that most plants have more immediate defenses than poison to discourage being eaten. Many poisonous plants smell bad, taste bad, or don't feel inviting, and this often serves as an early warning.

Rosalind Creasy's books, *Cooking from the Garden* and *The Complete Book of Edible Landscaping*, contain considerable detailed information about all aspects of this subject.

Edible Plants: Sources

This information is included as a quick reference to a wide variety of edible plantings. It is suggested that the following sources be consulted for much more complete information, especially regarding edible blossoms.

This sketch shows a good Xeriscape design (reduced lawn area of low water demand grass, with zoned shrub and flower plantings). The labels indicate existing plants and suggest alternatives. It would still be water efficient, but would also be edible and attractive to wildlife.

Existing: Honeylocust
Alt: Mulberry, Black Walnut, or Kentucky Coffee Tree

Existing: crabapple
Alt: apricot, peach, tart cherry

Existing: Turf-type Tall Fescue lawn
Introduce: clover and feed to rabbits

Unmowed meadow grasses, good cover for wildlife

Existing: fence
Add: a grape vine

Existing: crabapple
Alt: semi-dwarf apple, pear, or plum

Existing: stepping stones
Add: thyme in the cracks

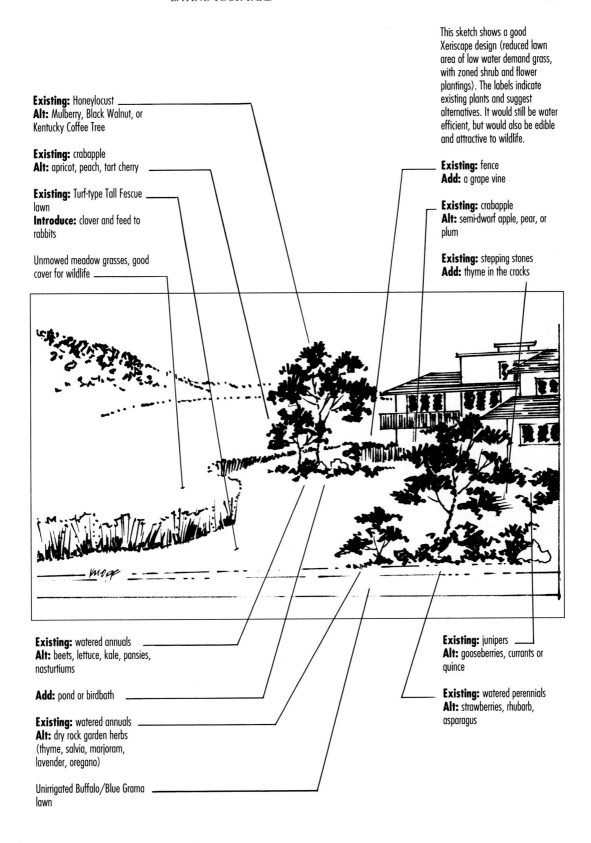

Existing: watered annuals
Alt: beets, lettuce, kale, pansies, nasturtiums

Add: pond or birdbath

Existing: watered annuals
Alt: dry rock garden herbs (thyme, salvia, marjoram, lavender, oregano)

Unirrigated Buffalo/Blue Grama lawn

Existing: junipers
Alt: gooseberries, currants or quince

Existing: watered perennials
Alt: strawberries, rhubarb, asparagus

Creasy, Rosalind. *The Complete Book of Edible Landscaping*. San Francisco: Sierra Club Books, 1982.

Creasy, Rosalind. *Cooking from the Garden: Creative Gardening and Contemporary Cooking*. San Francisco: Sierra Club Books, 1988.

Creasy, Rosalind. "Carrot Tops, Radish Blossoms, Pea Tendrils, and Other Overlooked Garden Treasures." *National Gardening*. July 1988.

Pleasant, Barbara. "Edible Bouquet." *Organic Gardening*. January 1989.

VEGETABLES, HERBS, SHRUBS, TREES, VINES, AND EDIBLE BLOSSOMS

Rated by watering zones

VEGETABLES

Allium spp.	Onions	M±
Apium graveolens	Celery	H
Asparagus officinalis	Asparagus	M±
Beta vulgaris	Beets	M,H
Brassica oleracea	Kale	M,H
Brassica spp.	Broccoli and Cauliflower	H
Brassica spp.	Cabbage and Brussel Sprouts	H
Capsicum spp.	Peppers	M,H
Cucumis spp.	Cucumbers and Melons	M,H
Cucurbita pepo	Squash	M,H
Daucus carota var. dulce	Carrots	M,H
Fragraria spp.	Strawberries	M,H
Lactuca sativa	Lettuce	H
Lycopersicon spp.	Tomatoes	M
Phaseolus spp.	Beans	M±
Pisum spp.	Peas	H
Raphanus sativus	Radishes	H
Solanum melongena	Eggplant	M,H
Solanum tuberosum	Potatoes	M,H
Zea Mays	Corn (Maize)	M,H

HERBS

Achillea spp.	Yarrow	L,M
Allium sativum	Garlic	M±
Allium schoenoprasum	Chives	M±
Anethum graveolens	Dill	M±
Armoracia rusticana	Horseradish	M±
Artemisia abrotanum	Southernwood	L,M
Artemisia dracunculus	Tarragon	M±
Borago officinalis	Borage	M±
Chamaemelum nobile	Chamomile	M±
Chrysanthemum parthenium	Feverfew	M±

EDIBLE PLANTS: A WORD TO THE WISE

"Learning taxonomy by taste," as one plantsman in Utah put it, can lead to serious consequences. Virginia Creeper *(Parthenocissus quinquefolia)*, for example, can create severe irritation in the digestive system of humans.

It is important to know exactly what plant is about to be tasted, as well as whether it is entirely safe—sometimes one part of a plant is ok, and another part is not. It is also important to know whether the plant has been sprayed with any harmful chemicals. When reading about ethnobotanical uses of plants, bear in mind that special treatment may be involved, and using proper amounts of various ingredients can be critical.

Fortunately, serious poisoning from either wild plants or landscape plants is quite rare. This is probably based on the fact that most people are naturally cautious, as well as the fact that most poisonous plants smell bad, taste bad, or don't feel inviting, and this often serves as an early warning.

Rosalind Creasy's books, *Cooking from the Garden*, and *The Complete Book of Edible Landscaping*, contain considerable detailed information about all aspects of this subject. ∎

Coriandrum sativum	Coriander	M±
Foeniculum spp.	Fennel	M±
Galium odoratum	Woodruff	M,H
Hyssopus officinalis	Hyssop	L,M
Lavandula spp.	Lavender	M±
Melissa officinalis	Lemon Balm	M±
Mentha spp.	Mint	M,H
Monarda spp.	Monarda	M,H
Ocimum basilicum	Basil	H
Origanum spp.	Marjoram	M±
Origanum spp.	Oregano	L,M
Petroselinum crispum	Parsley	M±
Rheum spp.	Rhubarb	M,H
Ruta graveolens	Rue	M±
Salvia officinalis	Sage	L,M
Santolina chamaecyparissus	Santolina	L,M
Symphytum officinale	Comfrey	M,H
Tanacetum vulgare	Tansy	M±
Teucrium spp.	Germander	L,M
Thymus spp.	Thyme	L,M
Tropaeolum majus	Nasturtium	M±
Verbascum thapsus	Mullein	L,M

SHRUBS

Amelanchier alnifolia	Rocky Mountain Serviceberry	M±
Chaenomeles spp.	Quince	M±
Cornus mas	Cornelian Cherry	M,H
Corylus spp.	Filberts and Hazelnuts	M,H
Hippophae rhamnoides	Sea Buckthorn	M,H
Mahonia spp.	Hollygrape species	L,M,H
Pinus edulis	Piñon Pine	L,M
Prunus americana	Wild Plum	M±
Prunus besseyi	Sand Cherry	M±
Prunus tomentosa	Nanking Cherry	M±
Prunus virginiana	Chokecherry	M±
Rhus spp.	Sumac species	L,M
Ribes spp.	Currant and Gooseberry species	M±
Rosa spp.	Rose species	M±
Rubus spp.	Raspberry and Blackberry species	M,H
Sambucus spp.	Elderberry species	H

TREES

Acer spp.	Maple species	M±
Diospyros virginiana	American Persimmon	M,H
Elaeagnus angustifolia	Russian Olive	M±
Juglans nigra	Black Walnut	M±
Malus spp.	Apple species	M,H
Morus spp.	Mulberry species	M±
Prunus armeniaca	Apricots	M,H

Prunus avium	Sweet Cherries	M,H
Prunus cerasus	Pie Cherries	M,H
Prunus domestica, Prunus salicina, Prunus insititida	Plums	M,H
Prunus persica	Peaches	M,H
Pyrus spp.	Pears	M,H

VINES

Humulus spp.	Hop species	M±
Vitis spp.	Grape species	M±

EDIBLE BLOSSOMS
Flowers, Trees, Shrubs, Vines, Herbs, and Vegetables

Agastache foeniculum	Anise Hyssop	M±
Alcea rosea	Hollyhock	M±
Allium schoenoprasum	Chives	M±
Begonia × tuberhybrida	Begonias	H
Borago officinalis	Borage	M±
Cercis canadensis	Red Bud	M±
Chrysanthemum × morifolium	Chrysanthemums	M±
Cichorium intybus	Chicory	M±
Cucurbita spp.	Squash blossoms	M±
Dianthus spp.	Pinks	M±
Hemerocallis spp.	Daylilies	M±
Hibiscus spp.	Hibiscus spp.	M,H
Lavandula spp.	Lavender	M±
Lonicera japonica	Honeysuckle	M,H
Malus spp.	Apple Blossoms	M±
Monarda spp.	Monarda	M,H
Ocimum basilicum	Basil flowers	H
Petunia × hybrida	Petunia	M±
Pisum sativum	Peas	H
Prunus spp.	Plums	M,H
Sambucus spp.	Elderberry flowers	H
Syringa spp.	Lilacs	M±
Tagetes spp.	Marigolds	M±
Tropaeolum majus	Nasturtiums	M±
Tulipa spp.	Tulip blossoms	L,M
Viola spp.	Violets and Pansies	H
Yucca spp.	Yucca blossoms	L,M

GRASSES FOR WATERWISE LAWNS

BUFFALOGRASS (Warm Season Grass)
Buchloë dactyloides

Water Requirements	0 to 3 gallons/square foot/20-week season. .5″ every two weeks for green grass in rainless weather.
Recovery from drought	This grass will make an excellent turf without irrigation, but light irrigation will keep it green, or will restore green quickly in very dry conditions. Too much water will encourage invasion by cool season grasses, with the possible exception of the new turf-type Buffalograss varieties.
Sun/shade requirements	Sun only.
Color	Distinctly bluegreen.
Texture	Very soft when actively growing.
Varieties	Native Buffalograss is shorter and requires less fertilizer than 'Texoka' or 'Sharps' varieties, which were developed for cattle forage. Treated seed is essential for rapid germination. 'Prairie' Buffalograss is one of several new turf-type Buffalograsses. It is a female cultivar that produces a very thick turf that has resisted invasion by cool season grasses, even when natural rainfall is high enough to cause considerable problems with wild or forage varieties. It must be planted as sprigs, plugs, or sod.
Growing season	Roughly from mid-May to early October in the Denver area.
Traffic tolerance	Tolerates considerable traffic. Grass blades will wear off during the winter, but regrow rapidly during the summer. Tolerates extremely compacted soil.
Mowing	Can be mowed at 1½ to 2 inches, or left to grow to height of 4 to 6 inches.
Establishment	**Seed** *Rate:* 2 to 3 lbs./1000 square feet. *Season:* Mid-May to mid-July (Denver area). *Hydromulch:* Recommended on large, windy, steep sites. *Watering:* 10 to 15 minutes, 3 times daily during germination. Every other day for 4 days. Every third day for 6 days. Once per week for a month, then every other week. More water will encourage weeds. *Weed control:* If needed, one application of a granulated broadleaf weed killer two or more months after germination. *Time to maturity:* One season with good conditions. **Sod** Blue Grama/Buffalograss sod in squares has been available in Colorado for several years. 'Prairie' and other turf-type varieties will probably be widely available soon. **Plugs** Plugs have also been available for several years in Colorado. Plugs and seed can be used together for quicker coverage.
Miscellaneous	The primary complaint with warm season grasses is about late green-up, and the visibility of cool season grasses within the Buffalograss early in the season. Mowing greatly reduces this problem. Buffalograss tends to produce a better turf on clay soil than on sandy soil. Fertilize with care —half the Bluegrass rate, once yearly, is a good estimate. Turf-type varieties may greatly reduce, or even eliminate, the problem of cool season grasses invading Buffalograss lawns. Selections may also be developed that will be more cold tolerant and more tolerant of short days in the fall. This will extend the growing season. Buffalograss is not considered to be salt-tolerant.

BLUE GRAMA (Warm Season Grass)

Bouteloua gracilis

Water Requirements	Same as Buffalograss.
Recovery from drought	Same as Buffalograss.
Sun/shade requirements	Sun only.
Color	Distinctly bluegreen.
Texture	Very soft when actively growing.
Varieties	Native, and several named varieties.
Growing season	Same as Buffalograss.
Traffic tolerance	Same as Buffalograss.
Mowing	Same as Buffalograss.
Establishment	**Seed** *Rate:* 2 to 3 lbs./1000 square feet. Same as Buffalograss.
	Season: Same as Buffalograss.
	Hydromulch: Same as Buffalograss.
	Watering: Same as Buffalograss.
	Weed control: Same as Buffalograss.
	Time to maturity: Same as Buffalograss.
	Sod Only available mixed with Buffalograss.
	Plugs Blue Grama is a bunch grass and won't spread from plugs.
Miscellaneous	As with Buffalograss, the main complaint is with the late start of growth in the spring. Spring bulbs have been successfully grown in both Buffalograss and Blue Grama. These include *Iris reticulata, Crocus spp., Narcissus asturiensis, Tulipa humilis, T. kolpakowskiana, T. linifolia, T. tarda,* and *T. urumiensis.* See "Splendor in the Grass," Sandy Snyder, *Fine Gardening.* May/June 1990. Both Blue Grama and Buffalograss do not want highly enriched soil. Too much nitrogen can be a problem.

CRESTED WHEATGRASS (Cool Season Grass)

Agropyron cristatum

Water Requirements	5 to 10 gallons/square foot/20-week season. .75" per week in hot, rainless weather.
Recovery from drought	This grass recovers very well from extended periods of very dry conditions. Without irrigation, however, it often produces a thin, bunchy lawn.
Sun/shade requirements	Sun or shade.
Color	Slightly bluer than Kentucky "Green" Grass.
Texture	At its best, this grass is indistinguishable from Kentucky Bluegrass. However, it normally produces a thinner lawn.
Varieties	'Fairway' and 'Ruff' were developed to create a more even turf than standard Crested Wheatgrass. 'Ephraim' is reported to spread slightly by rhizomes.
Growing season	Slightly longer than Kentucky Bluegrass.
Traffic tolerance	Moderate.
Mowing	Can be mowed like Kentucky Bluegrass, but it will be deeper rooted and more drought tolerant if mowed higher. This grass grows rapidly in the spring, and slows down considerably in hot weather. Most significantly, this grass can be allowed to grow to full height of 12 to 18 inches, then cut down to a traditional lawn height. The following season it can be allowed to grow to full height again.
Establishment	**Seed** *Rate:* 5 lbs./1000 square feet.

        Season: Same as Kentucky Bluegrass.

        Hydromulch: Same as other grasses.

        Watering: Same as Kentucky Bluegrass.

        Weed control: Same as other grasses.

        Time to maturity: First year, complete coverage, but thin. Second year, more complete coverage. It often takes several years to reach full density. Reseeding of bare spots is often needed.

Sod Not available.

Plugs Not available.

TURF-TYPE TALL FESCUE (Cool Season Grass)

Festuca varieties

Water Requirements	10± gallons/square foot/20-week season. .75" per week in hot, rainless weather.
Recovery from drought	Very good recovery from very dry conditions.
Sun/shade requirements	Sun or shade.
Color	Same as Kentucky Bluegrass.
Texture	A little more "coarse" than Kentucky Bluegrass.
Varieties	For lawns (thinner blades and darker green than other Tall Fescue varieties): Olympic, Apache, Jaguar, Adventure, Falcon, Mustang, Houndog, Arid. For meadows (wider blades, lighter green color): Fawn, Alta, Kentucky 31.
Growing season	Same as Kentucky Bluegrass.
Traffic tolerance	Same as Kentucky Bluegrass.
Mowing	1½ to 3 inches, a little higher than Kentucky Bluegrass.
Fertilizer	Less than Kentucky Bluegrass, possibly ½ to ¾ less.
Establishment	**Seed** *Rate:* 5 to 10 lbs./1000 square feet. *Season:* Same as Kentucky Bluegrass. *Hydromulch:* Same as Kentucky Bluegrass. *Watering:* Same as Kentucky Bluegrass the first year. *Weed Control:* Same as other grasses. *Time to maturity:* Usually one year. **Sod** Increasingly available. Often mixed with Kentucky Bluegrass. Pure Turf-type Tall Fescue sod has proved to be very successful, but sod that is a mixture of Turf-type Tall Fescue and Bluegrass has frequently been dominated by the Bluegrass. **Plugs** This is a bunch grass, and thus will not spread from plugs. It will also not spread into nearby gardens!
Miscellaneous	Turf-type Tall Fescue is considered to be one of the most salt-tolerant grasses. Some specialists consider it to be more shade-tolerant than Kentucky Bluegrass.

KENTUCKY BLUEGRASS (Cool Season Grass)

Poa pratensis varieties

Water Requirements	18 to 20 gallons/square foot/20-week season. .5″ three times/week in ordinary summer weather.
Recovery from drought	This grass suffers very quickly from heat and drought. It requires about two weeks to recover from a fully brown condition, and the turf will often suffer significant damage if unwatered for much more than a month in midsummer.
Sun/shade requirements	Sun or shade.
Color	Dark green.
Texture	Soft.
Varieties	Numerous varieties with varying sun/shade requirements and disease tolerance.
Growing season	In Denver, usually turns green in late March, with first mowing in mid-April. Gradually turns brown by mid-November, but variable weather can alter this significantly.
Traffic tolerance	Very good with sun and lots of water and fertilizer.
Mowing	1½ to 2 inches, twice weekly in midseason is common—unlike Buffalo-grass, Blue Grama, or Crested Wheatgrass lawns, which need only infrequent mowing.
Establishment	**Seed** *Rate:* 2 to 4 lbs./1000 square feet.

> **Seed** *Rate:* 2 to 4 lbs./1000 square feet.
> *Season:* April to August, but watering can be a problem in summer.
> *Hydromulch:* Same as other grasses.
> *Watering:* three times daily for germination, then enough to keep soil moist. Suffers more quickly than Blue Grama or Buffalograss if watering is inadequate.
> *Weed control:* Same as other grasses.
> *Time to maturity:* Complete coverage first year, mature turf during second year.

Sod Available from many sources.

Plugs Not available.

Sources of Seeds & Plants

Native Seeds/SEARCH
2509 N. Campbell Avenue, #325
Tucson, Arizona 85719
(602) 327-9123
Associated with the Tucson Botanic
Garden. Quarterly newsletter. An extensive list of native and historic seeds for
edible crops. Price list $1.00.

Seeds West Garden Seeds
Box 1739
El Prado, New Mexico 87529
A very pleasant, informative mail-order
catalog. Includes mostly well-selected vegetable varieties for the Rocky Mountain
region. Catalog $2.00.

Southwestern Native Seeds
Box 50503
Tucson, Arizona 85703
An extensive list of southwestern desert
and southwestern high-country seeds.
Mail-order seed catalog $1.00.

North Plan Seed Producers
Box 9107
Moscow, Idaho 83843
(208) 882-8040
A good selection of western native seeds.
Mail order.

New Mexico Native Plant Nursery
907 Pope Street
Silver City, New Mexico 88061
(505) 538-5201
Mostly local native seeds and live plants.
Retail and wholesale. Mail-order catalog.

Seeds of Change
1364 Rufina Circle #5
Santa Fe, New Mexico 87501
(505) 438-8080
Extensive offering of regionally adapted
seeds.

Bernardo Beach Native Plant Farm
1 Sanchez Road
Star Route 7, Box 145
Vequita, New Mexico 87062
(505) 345-6248
also:
520 Montaño N.W.
Albuquerque, New Mexico 87107
(505) 345-6248
An excellent assortment of native plants
and seeds. Mail order and on-site sales.

Mesa Garden
Box 72
Belen, New Mexico 87002
(505) 864-3131
An extensive list of North American
cactus and southern African plants and
seeds. Catalog $.50.

Plants of the Southwest
Agua Fria
Rt. 6 Box 11-A
Santa Fe, New Mexico 87501
(505) 438-8888
Retail store is located in Agua Fria, $1/4$ mile
south of Siler Road.
also:
6670 Fourth Street N.W.
Albuquerque, New Mexico 87107
(505) 344-8830
A wonderful, well-illustrated catalog
with considerable cultural information
and numerous color photos. Many southwestern wildflowers, shrubs, trees, and
crop plants. Live plants and seeds. Wholesale and retail. Mail order and in-store
sales. Catalog $1.50.

Siskiyou Rare Plant Nursery
2825 Cummings Road
Medford, Oregon 97501
(503) 722-6846
An excellent selection of alpine and waterwise plants from around the world. Live plants. Mail order. Catalog $2.00.

Rocky Mountain Rare Plants
Box 20483
Denver, Colorado 80220
An extensive list of Alpine and waterwise seeds. Mail order. Catalog $1.00.

Thompson and Morgan
Box 1308
Jackson, New Jersey 08527
(908) 363-9356
An extensive list of common and unusual seeds. Well-illustrated catalog. Mail order.

Jim and Jenny Archibald
"Bryn Collen"
Ffostrasol, Llandysul
Dyfed, SA 44 55 B
Wales, U.K.
An extensive list of unusual tethyan seeds (especially from Turkey, central Asia, northern Africa, and Europe).

Agua Fria Nursery
1409 Agua Fria
Santa Fe, New Mexico 87501
(505) 938-4831
A wonderful selection of waterwise plants. Retail at the nursery.

Green Acres Nursery
4990 McIntyre Street
Golden, Colorado 80401
(303) 279-8204
An extensive offering of waterwise and conventional plants. Capable of propagating plants on special request. Wholesale only.

Soil Conservation Society of America
7515 N.E. Akeny Road
Akeny, Iowa 50021
(515) 289-2331
Directory lists nearly 250 different sources of native shrubs, trees, seeds, and nursery stock.

American Penstemon Society
1569 South Holland Court
Lakewood, Colorado 80226
Seed and plant exchanges. Newsletter with membership. Exact address is likely to change with new officers, so check at a local botanic garden library for latest address.

Wild Bird Center
826 Pearl Street
Boulder, Colorado 80302
(303) 442-1322
Custom butterfly and hummingbird meadow mixes, plus extensive offerings of books, feeders, and other wildlife items. Retail at the store or mail order. Catalog $2.00.

Edible Landscaping
Box 77
Afton, Virginia 80436
(804) 361-9134
An intriguing list of unusual and common edible plants. An appealing catalog.

Raintree Nursery
391 Butts Road
Morton, Washington 98356
(206) 496-6400
An extremely informative catalog. Wide assortment emphasizing fruits, nuts, and berries.

Stark Bros Nurseries
Louisiana, Missouri 63353
(800) 325-4180
A well-illustrated catalog. Extensive offerings. Primarily fruits, nuts, and berries.

Prairie Nursery
Box 306
Westfield, Wisconsin 53964
(608) 296-3679
An informative catalog. Emphasis on midwestern prairie plants. Seeds and live plants. Mail order. Catalog $2.00.

Wild Seed
2073 East ASU Circle
Tempe, Arizona 85284
(602) 345-0669
Supply and contract collection of native American seed. Limited retail. Mail order. Catalog $2.00.

McClure and Zimmerman
108 West Winnebago
Box 368
Friesland, Wisconsin 53935
(414) 326-5769
An extensive offering of bulbs, corms, tubers, and root stocks, including many of the wonderful central Asian waterwise crocus, tulips, alliums, fritillaria, and so on. Mail order. Well-illustrated catalog.

Kurt Bluemel, Inc.
Rare Plant Division
2740 Greene Lane
Baldwin, Maryland 21013
An extensive offering of rare plants and seeds. Plant list $2.00.

Prairie Seed Source
Box 83
North Lake, Wisconsin 53064
A wide assortment of midwestern prairie plants, many of which extend to the foothills of the Rocky Mountains. Catalog $1.00.

Nichols Garden Nursery
1190 North Pacific Highway
Albany, Oregon 97321
(503) 967-8406
An impressive offering that emphasizes seeds for herbs and other edible plants.

High Altitude Gardens
Box 4619
Ketchum, Idaho 83340
Many selected varieties of crop plants and wildflowers for high altitudes and northern locations. Seeds. Mail order. Catalog $2.00, refundable.

Seeds Blüm
Idaho City Stage
Boise, Idaho 83706
Selected heirloom varieties of vegetables, including edible blossoms. Catalog $2.00.

Sander Seed Company
Box 271
Grand Junction, Colorado 81502
(303) 241-7660
Custom native seed mixes for the Rocky Mountain region.

Edge of the Rockies
Native Plants and Seeds
133 Hunna Road
Bayfield, Colorado 81122
A good selection of regional native plants with very helpful cultural information. Catalog $1.00.

Local Native Plant Societies
These groups sometimes have local plant sales as well as plant and seed exchanges. See Xeriscape & Native Plant Organizations for addresses of specific Rocky Mountain states native plant societies.

Public Xeriscape Demonstration Areas

A word to the wise is in order when observing public Xeriscape demonstration areas. Due to mistakes in design, construction, and maintenance, these areas are frequently less than perfect. There is much to learn from them, however, if observations are made carefully.

Arizona

The Arboretum at Flagstaff
South Woody Mountain Road
Box 670
Flagstaff, Arizona 86002
(602) 774-1441
Two hundred acres of existing native plantings, including shrubs, trees, wildflowers, and meadows. Emphasis on horticulture related to the Colorado Plateau. Several new Xeriscape plantings in progress. Newsletter with membership.

Colorado

Boulder Creek Xeriscape Garden
Between the Boulder Creek Trail and
Canyon Boulevard at the Justice Center.
Boulder, Colorado.
Flowers, shrubs, and turf areas.

Boulder Creek Peace Garden
On Boulder Creek near the public library.
Boulder, Colorado.
A considerable number of semiarid central Asian (Tethyan) native plants.

The Chautauqua Rangers' Cottage
Chautauqua Park
Boulder, Colorado
A well-labeled garden of plants native to the mountain edge of Boulder. One area emphasizes native plants for butterflies.

City of Arvada Public Works Center
6161 Olde Wadsworth Boulevard
Arvada, Colorado
(303) 420-0984
An extensive area devoted to Xeriscape shrubs, trees, groundcovers, flowers, and good use of Turf-type Tall Fescue lawn.

Colorado Springs Mesa Treatment Plant
2855 Mesa Road
Colorado Springs, Colorado
(719) 520-0300
A very comprehensive xeriscape demonstration garden in a spectacular location. Opening in the spring of 1991.

Career Enrichment Park
7330 Lowell Boulevard
Westminster, Colorado
(303) 428-2600
Features three watering zones, and includes lawns, flowers, and shrubs. Constructed with help from local high school students.

Denver Water Department
1600 West 12th Avenue
Denver, Colorado
(303) 628-6329 (call for directions)
An extensive demonstration garden including shrubs, trees, groundcovers, flowers, and turf. Major new areas planned for 1991.

Denver Botanic Gardens
1005 York Street
Denver, Colorado
(303) 331-4000
Xeriscape-relevant plantings include the Rock Alpine Garden, a ridge and rock outcrop area, and several carefully developed Great Plains grassland ecosystems.

Denver Botanic Gardens' Chatfield Arboretum
9201 South Carr Street
Littleton, Colorado
(303) 973-3705
A xeriscape garden for wildlife surrounding two former farmhouses. Under construction in 1991.

Douglas County Executive Building
101 Third Street
Castle Rock, Colorado
(303) 688-3096
Groundcovers, flowers, shrubs, and Turf-type Tall Fescue grass.

Longmont Public Library
Third and Kimbark
Longmont, Colorado
(303) 651-8360
Numerous ornamental grasses, flowers, shrubs, and groundcovers.

Oxley Homestead
Genesee Foundation
24425 West Currant Drive
Golden, Colorado 80401
(303) 526-0284
The entire Genesee area offers good examples of suburban development within a Ponderosa Pine ecosystem. The rock garden at the Oxley Homestead displays numerous native plants and is well labeled.

Fort Collins Xeriscape Demonstration Garden
Fort Collins City Hall
300 La Porte Avenue
Fort Collins, Colorado
(303) 221-6681
An elaborate display of flowers, shrubs, trees, groundcovers, and turf.

Kansas

Botanica (the Wichita Gardens)
701 Amidon
Wichita, Kansas 67203
(316) 264-0448
Xeriscape plantings include turf, shrubs, trees, and flowers. Well-considered plant lists available.

Nevada

Benson Garden
University of Nevada, Reno
(located on campus)
A xeriscape demonstration area with shrubs, trees, and groundcovers labeled.

Sierra Plaza Xeriscape Demonstration Garden
Water Utility Headquarters
6100 Neil Road
Reno, Nevada
A public xeriscape garden with flowers, shrubs, trees, groundcovers, and turf demonstrations. Plans include signs and interpretive information.

New Mexico

Albuquerque Xeriscape Demonstration Garden
Osuna and Wyoming
Parks and Recreation Department
(505) 768-3550
A sophisticated design including shrubs, flowers, groundcovers, lawns, and meadows. Under construction in 1991.

Santa Fe, New Mexico
The entire city offers many examples of landscaping with wonderful western plants. The area is especially spectacular between mid-September and mid-October when rabbitbrush, asters, groundsel, and Maximilian's Sunflower are in full bloom. This is an example of a largely lawnless city, and it's extremely appealing to the eye.

Utah

Red Butte Gardens and Arboretum
University of Utah
Building 436
Salt Lake City, Utah 84111
(801) 581-5322
An arboretum and gardens emphasizing intermountain horticulture. Native plant areas and xeriscape plantings, with interpretive information, are either planned or in place.

Xeriscape & Native Plant Organizations

Arizona

The Arboretum at Flagstaff
South Woody Mountain Road
Box 670
Flagstaff, Arizona 86002
(602) 744-1441

Colorado

American Penstemon Society
Membership Secretary
1569 South Holland Court
Lakewood, Colorado 80226

**Associated Landscape
Contractors of Colorado**
Wheatridge, Colorado
(303) 425-4862

**City of Colorado Springs
Water Division**
30 South Nevada, Suite 603
Box 1103
Colorado Springs, Colorado 80947

City of Arvada Utilities Division
8101 Ralston Road
Arvada, Colorado 80002
(303) 431-3035

**City of Aurora
Water Utilities Department**
1470 South Havana, Suite 400
Aurora, Colorado 80012
(303) 695-7381

**City of Fort Collins
Water Utilities Department**
Fort Collins City Hall
300 La Porte Avenue
Fort Collins, Colorado 80522
(303) 221-6688

**City of Boulder
Department of Public Works**
Box 791
Boulder, Colorado 80306
(303) 441-4243

Colorado State University
Cooperative Extension
Jefferson County Office
(303) 277-8980

U.S.D.A. Soil Conservation Service
Metro Denver Office
(303) 236-2702

Colorado Native Plant Society
Box 200
Fort Collins, Colorado 80502

Colorado Nurseryman's Association
(800) 237-7386

Denver Botanic Gardens
1005 York Street
Denver, Colorado 80206
(303) 331-4000

Denver Water Department
1600 West 12th Avenue
Denver, Colorado 80254
(303) 628-6329

**Metro Water Conservation, Inc.
and Xeriscape Colorado**
Contact the Denver Water Department
(303) 628-6329

**Colorado Chapter, American
Society of Landscape Architects**
Denver, Colorado
(303) 830-0094

Idaho

Idaho Native Plant Society
Box 9451
Boise, Idaho 83707

Kansas

Botanica (the Wichita Gardens)
701 Amidon
Wichita, Kansas 67203
(316) 264-0448

Montana

Montana Native Plant Society
Box 92
Bozeman, Montana 59771

Nevada

Northern Nevada Native Plant Society
Box 8965
Reno, Nevada 89507

New Mexico

Native Plant Society of New Mexico
Box 5917
Santa Fe, New Mexico 87502

Santa Fe Metropolitan Water Board
Box 276
Santa Fe, New Mexico 87501
(505) 984-5010

City of Albuquerque
Parks Management Department
Box 1293
Albuquerque, New Mexico 87103
(505) 768-3550

Oregon

Native Plant Society of Oregon
c/o Department of Biology
Southern Oregon State College
Ashland, Oregon 97520

Texas

The National Xeriscape Council, Inc.
President, Doug Welsh
Texas Agricultural Extension Service
225 Horticulture/Forestry Building
College Station, Texas 77843
(409) 845-7341

National Wildflower Research Center
2600 FM 973 North
Austin, Texas 78725
(512) 929-3600

Utah

Center for Plant Conservation
State Arboretum of Utah
University of Utah
Salt Lake City, Utah 84111
(801) 581-5322

Utah Botanic Gardens
1817 North Main Street
Farmington, Utah 84025

Washington

Washington Native Plant Society
Seattle, Washington 98195
(206) 543-1942

ANNOTATED BIBLIOGRAPHY

Horticulture & Design

Armitage, Allan M.
1989   *Herbaceous Perennial Plants: A Treatise on Their Identification, Culture and Garden Attributes.* Athens: Varsity Press, Inc.
A very comprehensive manual of perennial garden plants. Focus is on gardening in the eastern United States, but there is much information of use to western gardeners.

Bailey, Liberty Hyde, Ethel Zoe, and staff of the Liberty Hyde Bailey Hortorium.
1976   *Hortus Third.* New York: MacMillan Publishing Company.
A very comprehensive dictionary of plants cultivated in the United States and Canada.

Borland, Jim, Sylvia B. Brockner, and Jeanne R. Janish.
1987   *Native Plants of Genesee and How to Use Them in Foothills Residential Landscape Design.* Golden: Genesee Foundation (24425 West Currant Drive, Golden, Colorado 80401).
A very useful guide to using Rocky Mountain foothills woody plants in residential landscaping.

Bowers, Janice Emily.
1987   *100 Roadside Wildflowers of Southwest Woodlands.* Tucson: Southwest Parks and Monuments Association.
Very good color photos, very good selection of wildflowers, and very interesting text.

Elmore, Francis H.
1976   *Shrubs and Trees of the Southwest Uplands.* Tucson: Southwest Parks and Monuments Association.
Good color photos, helpful drawings, and very informative text.

Harper, Pamela, and Frederick McGourty.
1983   *Perennials: How to Select, Grow, and Enjoy.* Tucson: HP Books.
A very useful guide to a good selection of garden perennials. Good color photos.

Kelly, George W.
1970   *A Guide to the Woody Plants of Colorado.* Boulder: Pruett Publishing Company.
Many good color photos, and very informative text. Covers many very useful Rocky Mountain native shrubs and trees.

Lamb, Larry.
1990   "A Tall-Grass Prairie in a Small Backyard." *Fine Gardening.* May/June.
A very specific article about creating and maintaining a tallgrass meadow in suburbia. Very helpful color photos.

Snyder, Sandy.
1990   "Splendor in the Grass: Spring Bulbs Brighten a Dormant
          Lawn." *Fine Gardening*. May/June.
A very informative article about using drought-tolerant flowering bulbs
in a Buffalograss lawn. Good color photos.

Proctor, Rob.
1990   *Perennials: Enduring Classics for the Contemporary Garden*.
          New York: Harper and Row.
A very well-illustrated book with a vast amount of historical
information about a wonderful selection of garden perennials.

Phillips, Judith.
1989   "Landscaping a Wide-open Space: Facing Up to Sand, Wind
          and Drought." *Fine Gardening*. November/December.
A very informative article on gardening in central New Mexico.

American Rock Garden Society and Denver Botanic Gardens.
1986   *Rocky Mountain Alpines*. Portland: Timber Press.
A very good book about alpine plants and rock gardening. Two chapters
devoted to propagation of plants.

Springer, Lauren.
1990   *Mountain, Plain and Garden: The Magazine of Denver Botanic
          Gardens*. Denver: Denver Botanic Gardens, Autumn/Winter.
Many very informative articles about waterwise plants and gardening.

Taylor, Ronald J., and Rolf W. Valum.
1974   *Wildflowers 2: Sagebrush Country*. Beaverton: The Touchstone
          Press.
Unusually good photos and informative text.

Smith, Robert J., and Beatrice S. Smith.
1980   *The Prairie Garden: 70 Native Plants You Can Grow in Town and
          Country*. Madison: University of Wisconsin Press.
Considerable cultural information about a good selection of Great Plains
grasslands plants.

Lamb, Samuel H.
1975   *Woody Plants of the Southwest*. Santa Fe: The Sunstone Press.
A very useful field guide with text, drawings, range maps, and photos.

Strauch, Jr., J.G., and J.E. Klett.
1989   *Flowering Herbaceous Perennials for the High Plains*. Ft. Collins:
          Colorado State University.
A very useful guide with very helpful color photos.

1979   *Sunset New Western Garden Book*. Menlo Park: Lane
          Publishing Co.
A superb, concise encyclopedia of western garden plants.

Welsh, Stanley L.
1987   *A Utah Flora*. Provo: Brigham Young University.
A very comprehensive manual of the vascular flora of Utah. Includes
ecological information and natural distribution by county.

Wosowski, Sally, and Andy Wosowski.
1988   *Native Texas Plants: Landscaping Region by Region*. Austin:
            Texas Monthly Press.
A very instructive guide to landscaping with native Texas plants.
Very good coverage of specific plants. Many color photos.

Phillips, Roger, and Martyn Rix.
1989   *The Random House Book of Bulbs*. New York: Random House.
A remarkably complete book with over 1,000 flowering bulbs of many
kinds, in color photos. Many plants are illustrated in their natural
habitat.

McGregor, Ronald L.
1986   *Flora of the Great Plains*. Lawrence: University Press of Kansas.
An extremely comprehensive manual of vascular plants known to be
native or naturalized in the Great Plains.

Xeriscape   1990   *At Home with Xeriscape*. Denver: Xeriscape Colorado.
A brochure with drawings and color photos.

Knox, Kimberly, ed.
1989   *Landscaping for Water Conservation: Xeriscape!* Aurora,
            Colorado: City of Aurora.
A book about xeriscaping in the Rocky Mountain region. Drawings,
color photos, and plant lists.

Phillips, Judith.
1987   *Southwestern Landscaping with Native Plants*. Santa Fe: Museum
            of New Mexico Press.
Excellent coverage of southwestern desert and high country plants.
Considerable detailed information about propagation and culture.
Numerous photos.

1989   *Sunset Waterwise Gardening*. Menlo Park: Lane Publishing Co.
Comprehensive coverage of water-efficient landscaping. Focus is on
southern California.

1990   *Taylor's Guide to Water-Saving Gardening*. Boston: Houghton
            Mifflin Company.
An extensive assortment of color photographs of a wide variety of
plants. Nationwide focus.

Wildlife   Carr, Anna.
Gardening   1979   *Rodale's Handbook of Garden Insects*. Emmaus: Rodale Press.
An excellent photographic guide for identifying common insects.

Damrosch, Barbara.
1982   *Theme Gardens*. New York: Workman Publishing
          Company, Inc.
A delightfully illustrated garden book, with a superb chapter on butterfly
gardening.

Hammerson, Geoffrey A.
1982   *Amphibians and Reptiles in Colorado*. Denver: Colorado Division
          of Wildlife.
An excellent photographic guide to identifying Colorado reptiles.

Henderson, Carroll L.
1981   *Landscaping for Wildlife*. St. Paul: Minnesota Department of
          Natural Resources (500 Lafayette Road, Box 7, St. Paul,
          Minnesota).
An uncommonly good general guide to wildlife habitat development.

Henderson, Carroll L.
n.d.   *Woodworking for Wildlife: Homes for Birds and Mammals*.
          St. Paul: Minnesota Department of Natural Resources.
An excellent source of detailed information about constructing shelters
for many wildlife species.

Merilees, Bill.
1989   *Attracting Backyard Wildlife: A Guide for Nature Lovers*.
          Stillwater: Voyageur Press.
An unusually good general guide for residential wildlife gardening.

McKinley, Michael.
1983   *How to Attract Birds*. San Francisco: Ortho/Chevron.
A very good guide for attracting birds to residential areas.

Stokes, Donald, and Lillian Stokes.
1987   *The Bird Feeder Book: An Easy Guide to Attracting, Identifying,
          and Understanding Your Feeder Birds*. Toronto: Little, Brown
          and Company.
Very well-presented information about feeding wildlife.

Tyrell, Esther, and Robert Tyrell.
1985   *Hummingbirds: Their Life and Behavior*. New York: Crown
          Publishers.
An extraordinary photographic book with very complete text.

Edible Landscaping

Creasy, Rosalind.
1988   *Cooking from the Garden: Creative Gardening and Contemporary
          Cooking*. San Francisco: Sierra Club Books.
An extraordinary cookbook with very good cultural information about
a wide array of edible plants. Extremely well-illustrated with color
photographs.

Creasy, Rosalind.
1982   *The Complete Book of Edible Landscaping*. San Francisco: Sierra
        Club Books.
A delightful book about home landscaping with food-bearing plants.

Phillips, Roger, and Ricky Fay.
1990   *The Random House Book of Herbs*. New York: Random House.
A vast amount of interesting information about a very large assortment
of herbal plants. Well-illustrated with color photos.

Stebbins, Robert L., and Lance Walheim.
1981   *Western Fruit, Berries and Nuts*. Tucson: HP Books.
A very useful source of information on a vast array of useful varieties of
fruit, berries, and nut-bearing plants.

Stuart, Malcolm.
1979   *Herbs and Herbalism*. New York: Van Nostrand Reinhold
        Company.
A remarkable amount of interesting information about a very large
assortment of herbal plants. Well-illustrated with color photos.

Tolley, Emelie, and Chris Mead.
1985   *Herbs: Gardens, Decorations and Recipes*. New York: Clarkson
        Potter, Inc. Publishers.
An extremely well-illustrated guide to herbs and use of herbs.

Natural & Cultural History

Kindscher, Kelly.
1987   *Edible Wildplants of the Prairie: An Ethnobotanical Guide*.
        Lawrence: University Press of Kansas.
A very helpful guide to ethnobotanical information about Great Plains
plants.

Moore, Michael.
1989   *Medicinal Plants of the Desert and Canyon West*. Santa Fe:
        Museum of New Mexico Press.
An extensive compilation of indigenous plants with medicinal and
other uses.

Moore, Michael.
1979   *Medicinal Plants of the Mountain West*. Santa Fe: Museum of
        New Mexico Press.
An extensive compilation of indigenous plants with medicinal and
other uses.

Mutel, Cornelia Fleischer, and John C. Emerick.
1984   *From Grassland to Glacier: The Natural History of Colorado*.
        Boulder: Johnson Books.
An extensive guide to the ecosystems of Colorado. Applicable throughout the Rocky Mountain region.

Benyus, Janine M.
1989   *The Field Guide to Wildlife Habitats of the Western United States.*
         New York: Simon & Schuster, Inc.
A delightfully illustrated, informative guide to ecosystems throughout
the western United States.

Van Bruggen, Theodore.
1983   *Wildflowers, Grasses and other Plants of the Northern Great Plains.*
         Interior, South Dakota: Badlands Natural History Association.
An extensive assortment of photographs. A good guide for quick
identification of Great Plains flora.

Johnson, James R., and James T. Nichols.
1970   *Plants of South Dakota Grasslands: A Photographic Study.*
         Brookings: Agricultural Experiment Station S.D. State
         University.
An excellent collection of photos and related text.

Cushman, Ruth Carol, and Stephen R. Jones.
1989   *The Shortgrass Prairie.* Boulder: Pruett Publishing Company.
Excellent photos and text covering the shortgrass portions of the Great
Plains.

Lanner, Ronald M.
1981   *The Piñon Pine: A Natural and Cultural History.* Reno:
         University of Nevada Press.
An interesting and informative book about the Piñon Pine and its
ecosystem.

PLANT INDEX

SUBJECT INDEX